Simply Ming™

STOVETOP OVEN
COOKBOOK

— *Simply Ming*™ —
STOVETOP OVEN
COOKBOOK
SIMPLY DELICIOUS HOMEMADE RECIPES

Cover and interior design by Katie Jennings Campbell
Layout by Tara Long

Castle Point Publishing
58 Ninth Street Hoboken, NJ 07030
www.castlepointpub.com

ISBN: 978-0-9982297-3-7

Printed and bound in the United States of America.

10 9 8 7 6 5 4 3 2 1

CONTENTS

7 | EASY APPETIZERS

29 | BEST BREAKFASTS AND BRUNCHES

59 | AMAZING MAINS

137 | DELICIOUS DESSERTS

158 | ALPHABETICAL LIST OF RECIPES

160 | METRIC CONVERSIONS

EASY
APPETIZERS

Cheesy SPINACH-ARTICHOKE DIP

CHEESY DIPS ARE ALWAYS A HIT. You'll love this one, which features fresh baby spinach and goes straight from burner to baking with the Simply Ming Stovetop Oven.

1 TABLESPOON OLIVE OIL

1 LARGE SHALLOT, MINCED

3 CLOVES GARLIC, MINCED

12 CUPS PACKED BABY SPINACH

1 CAN (14 OUNCES) ARTICHOKE HEARTS, RINSED AND COARSELY CHOPPED

1 CUP RICOTTA CHEESE

1/4 CUP SOUR CREAM

1/4 CUP MAYONNAISE

1 CUP GRATED PARMESAN CHEESE, DIVIDED

1 TABLESPOON FRESH LEMON JUICE

1/2 TEASPOON KOSHER SALT

3/4 TEASPOON FRESHLY GROUND BLACK PEPPER

3/4 CUP CRUMBLED FETA CHEESE

1. Preheat the oven to 400°F. Warm the pan over medium heat, then add the oil. Add the shallot and cook for about 2 minutes or until golden. Add the garlic and spinach and continue cooking until the spinach has wilted, about 2 minutes. Remove from the heat.

2. Pour off the excess moisture from the spinach mixture. Add the artichoke hearts, ricotta cheese, sour cream, mayonnaise, ½ cup of the Parmesan, lemon juice, salt, and pepper. Combine well and smooth the top. Sprinkle on the feta cheese and remaining ½ cup Parmesan.

3. Bake for 35 to 40 minutes or until golden brown. Let cool for 10 minutes. Serve with pita chips or crostini.

Warm
FRENCH ONION DIP

YOU CAN HAVE THE FLAVOR of French onion soup in a dip that pairs perfectly with crostini. The blend of caramelized onions and gooey cheese will tempt you to eat it right out of the pan.

1 TABLESPOON REFINED OLIVE OIL

1 TABLESPOON CLARIFIED BUTTER

2 VIDALIA ONIONS, SLICED INTO THIN RINGS

2 CLOVES GARLIC, MINCED

1 CUP SOUR CREAM

1/2 CUP MAYONNAISE

1 CUP SHREDDED GRUYERE CHEESE

KOSHER SALT AND FRESHLY GROUND BLACK PEPPER

1. Preheat the oven to 400°F. Warm the pan over medium heat, then add the oil and butter. Add the onions and cook for about 5 minutes. Reduce the heat to low and cook, stirring often, until the onions turn a deep golden brown, 20 to 25 minutes.

2. Add the garlic and cook for 1 minute. Remove from the heat.

3. In a medium bowl, combine the sour cream and mayonnaise. Add the sour cream mixture, Gruyere, salt, and pepper to the onion mixture in the pan; mix well. Bake for 20 minutes or until bubbly and browned on top. Serve with crostini.

Scallop CAPRESE STACKS

A SIMPLE INGREDIENT SWAP ELEVATES your traditional caprese stacks. Just sub tender sautéed scallops for the mozzarella. You won't add much time or effort at all, because scallops cook so quickly and the Simply Ming Stovetop Oven cleans up with ease.

---

1 CUP BALSAMIC VINEGAR

1 CLOVE GARLIC, CRUSHED

4 TABLESPOONS OLIVE OIL, DIVIDED

12 SEA SCALLOPS (ABOUT 1½ POUNDS), CUT IN HALF HORIZONTALLY

KOSHER SALT AND FRESHLY GROUND BLACK PEPPER

3 LARGE TOMATOES, CUT INTO SLICES ABOUT ¼ INCH THICK

1 OR 2 AVOCADOS, PEELED AND THINLY SLICED

BASIL, FOR GARNISH

1. In the pan over medium heat, add the balsamic vinegar and garlic. Bring to a boil. Reduce the heat to low and simmer until the liquid has reduced to about half. Remove the liquid and set aside.

2. Rewarm the pan over medium heat, then add 1 tablespoon of the oil.

3. Brush the scallops with the remaining 3 tablespoons oil and season with salt and pepper. Add the scallops to the pan, and sauté until firm and opaque, about 2 minutes per side.

4. To serve, place the tomato slices on a serving plate. Layer each with a scallop half, avocado slice, scallop half, and tomato slice. Drizzle with the balsamic reduction. Garnish with basil.

Simple
CHICKEN YAKITORI

A SWEET AND SAVORY GLAZE and juicy chicken thighs make this an easy appetizer to master. It's sure to please company but can also be enjoyed as a light meal on its own. The Simply Ming Stovetop Oven Pan makes basting simple.

2/3 CUP REDUCED-SODIUM SOY SAUCE

1/2 CUP SAKE

1/4 CUP MIRIN

1/2 CUP DARK BROWN SUGAR

1 TEASPOON MINCED FRESH GINGER

1 CLOVE GARLIC, MINCED

2 POUNDS SKINLESS, BONELESS CHICKEN THIGHS, CUT INTO 1-INCH PIECES

2 TABLESPOONS PEANUT OIL

KOSHER SALT AND FRESHLY GROUND PEPPER TO TASTE

SCALLIONS, THINLY SLICED, FOR GARNISH

1. In the pan over medium heat, whisk together the soy sauce, sake, mirin, sugar, ginger, and garlic. Bring to a boil, stirring occasionally, until the sauce is slightly thickened, about 20 minutes.

2. Soak 8 bamboo skewers in water for 20 minutes; drain. Thread the chicken onto the skewers and brush with the oil. Season with salt and pepper.

3. Transfer 1 cup of the sauce to a bowl to reserve for dipping.

4. Insert the rack for the pan. Warm the pan over medium heat. Place the chicken skewers on the rack and grill, turning, until just cooked through, about 10 minutes. Baste with the sauce in the pan several times during grilling. Garnish with scallions. Serve with the reserved sauce.

Chili-Lime
SHRIMP SKEWERS

SWEET AND HEAT MEET IN THE MARINADE for these shrimp skewers. And now you can easily grill them on your stovetop any time of year with the rack insert for the Simply Ming Stovetop Oven.

3 TABLESPOONS FRESH LIME JUICE

2 TABLESPOONS OLIVE OIL

1 TABLESPOON WHITE WINE VINEGAR

1 TABLESPOON CHOPPED FRESH CILANTRO LEAVES

2 TABLESPOONS SWEET CHILI SAUCE

2 CLOVES GARLIC, MINCED

1/2 TABLESPOON HONEY

1/2 TEASPOON KOSHER SALT

1/4 TEASPOON FRESHLY GROUND BLACK PEPPER

1/4 TEASPOON RED PEPPER FLAKES

1 POUND PEELED AND DEVEINED SHRIMP, TAILS ON

1. Soak 8 bamboo skewers in water for 20 minutes; drain.

2. In a large bowl, mix the lime juice, olive oil, vinegar, cilantro, chili sauce, garlic, honey, salt, pepper, and red pepper flakes. Add the shrimp and toss to coat evenly. Marinate in the refrigerator for 30 minutes.

3. Thread the shrimp onto the skewers.

4. Insert the rack for the pan. Warm the pan over medium heat. Place the shrimp skewers on the rack and grill for 5 to 8 minutes or until the shrimp turn pink, turning once.

Vegetable STUFFED MUSHROOMS

LOOKING FOR A HEARTIER START? Mushrooms stuffed with chopped vegetables and topped with melted mozzarella please palates and won't keep you in the kitchen very long.

2 TEASPOONS OLIVE OIL, DIVIDED

12 LARGE WHITE MUSHROOMS, STEMS REMOVED AND RESERVED

1/2 CUP CHOPPED BABY SPINACH

1/2 ONION, MINCED

2 CLOVES GARLIC, CHOPPED

1/2 CUP CHERRY TOMATOES, CHOPPED

2 TABLESPOONS CHOPPED FRESH PARSLEY

1/8 TEASPOON KOSHER SALT

PINCH OF FRESHLY GROUND BLACK PEPPER

1/2 CUP SHREDDED MOZZARELLA CHEESE

1. Preheat the oven to 325°F. Brush a baking sheet with 1 teaspoon of the oil.

2. Finely chop the mushroom stems and set aside. Place the mushroom caps on the prepared baking sheet and bake for 12 minutes. Set aside.

3. Warm the pan over medium heat, then add the remaining 1 teaspoon oil. Add the mushroom stems, spinach, onion, and garlic, and sauté until the spinach wilts, about 2 minutes. Add the tomatoes and cook for 2 minutes more. Remove from the heat and stir in the parsley, salt, and pepper.

4. Heat the broiler. Divide the spinach mixture evenly among the mushroom caps. Sprinkle each with the mozzarella, then broil until browned, 2 to 3 minutes.

Skillet
SMOKY SALSA

CHARRING THE VEGETABLES FOR THIS SALSA brings out more flavor and adds a light touch of smokiness you'll love. Adjust the spice level by experimenting with more or less garlic and peppers. Jalapeños can replace the serranos.

3 ROMA TOMATOES, QUARTERED

3 CLOVES GARLIC, PEELED

2 SERRANO PEPPERS, STEMMED AND HALVED

1 MEDIUM ONION, CUT INTO WEDGES

1 TEASPOON GROUND CUMIN

3/4 TEASPOON KOSHER SALT

1/3 CUP CHOPPED FRESH CILANTRO

1 1/2 TABLESPOONS FRESH LIME JUICE

1. Warm the pan over medium heat. Add the tomatoes, cut-side down, garlic, and peppers. Cook, turning occasionally, for about 6 minutes or until slightly charred and softened. Remove from the heat and set aside. Add the onion wedges to the pan, and cook for 5 to 6 minutes or until slightly charred and softened.

2. Transfer the vegetables to a food processor fitted with a metal blade. Add the cumin and salt. Process to the desired consistency. Add the cilantro and lime juice, and pulse until just combined. Allow to cool. Serve at room temperature, or refrigerate in an airtight container for up to 3 days. Serve with tortilla chips.

Bacon-Wrapped
AVOCADO BITES

CRISPY BACON PAIRS WITH CREAMY AVOCADO in this easy appetizer. Just four ingredients serve up lots of flavor. Be more generous with the chili powder to add heat.

---

6 BACON STRIPS

1 AVOCADO, PEELED AND CUT INTO CHUNKS

1/3 CUP DARK BROWN SUGAR

1/2 TEASPOON CHILI POWDER

1. Insert the rack for the pan. Warm the pan over medium heat with the cover on.

2. Cut each slice of bacon into thin strips and wrap around the avocado pieces.

3. In a small bowl, mix together the brown sugar and chili powder. Roll the bacon bundles in the brown sugar mixture and place on the grill rack. Cover and cook for 10 to 15 minutes, turning halfway through. Remove from the heat. Stick a toothpick in each for serving.

Thai SALMON SLIDERS

SPICE UP SALMON SLIDERS WITH THAI FLAVOR. It doesn't take a lot of time or complicated ingredients. Your Simply Ming Stovetop Oven cooks up the patties beautifully.

---

1 EGG

1 TABLESPOON REDUCED-SODIUM SOY SAUCE

1 TABLESPOON SWEET CHILI SAUCE

¼ CUP CHOPPED FRESH CILANTRO

¼ CUP CHOPPED SCALLIONS

1 TEASPOON LIME ZEST

12-OUNCE SALMON FILLET, SKIN REMOVED, FINELY CHOPPED

½ CUP WHOLE WHEAT BREAD CRUMBS

1 TABLESPOON OLIVE OIL

6 SLIDER ROLLS

1. In a bowl, whisk the egg until lightly beaten. Stir in the soy sauce and sweet chili sauce. Add the cilantro, scallions, lime zest, salmon, and bread crumbs and gently fold just until combined.

2. Divide the mixture into 6 equal parts. Roll into balls and press slightly to form 6 small patties in all.

3. Warm the pan over medium heat, then add the oil. Cook the patties for 8 minutes, turning once, or until the fish is opaque. Serve on slider rolls.

Honey-Glazed GRILLED PINEAPPLE

SOMETIMES A LIGHTER BITE WILL DO. For an elegant fruit appetizer, pair pineapple with just the right accents and grilling technique to intensify its sweet flavor. So simple, so good!

1/3 CUP HONEY

1/4 CUP FRESH LIME JUICE

1/4 CUP ORANGE JUICE

1 LARGE RIPE PINEAPPLE, CORED, PEELED, AND SLICED

FRESH MINT, FOR GARNISH

1. In a large bowl, combine the honey, lime juice, and orange juice. Add the pineapple and turn to coat. Cover with plastic wrap; marinate at room temperature for 30 minutes.

2. Insert the rack for the pan. Warm the pan over medium heat. Remove the pineapple from the marinade. Place on the rack and grill until browned, 3 to 5 minutes per side. Serve warm or chilled. Garnish with mint.

Red Pepper and Asparagus QUESADILLAS

SPEED UP YOUR PREP TIME by using jarred roasted red peppers, or you can make your own using the directions in the Roasted Red Pepper Dip recipe on page 25.

---

1 TABLESPOON OLIVE OIL

1/4 POUND ASPARAGUS, TRIMMED AND CHOPPED

1/2 RED ONION, CHOPPED

1/2 CUP ROASTED RED PEPPERS, COARSELY CHOPPED

4 TORTILLAS

1/2 CUP SHREDDED MOZZARELLA CHEESE

1. Warm the pan over medium heat, then add the oil. Add the asparagus and onion and cook for 5 minutes, until tender. Add the peppers and cook for 1 minute. Transfer to a covered bowl to keep warm.

2. Reduce the heat to low. Warm a tortilla in the pan for 1 minute. Flip, sprinkle with 1 tablespoon cheese, one-fourth of the vegetable mixture, and then 1 tablespoon cheese; fold the tortillas in half. Cook for 4 minutes, flip, then cook for 2 more minutes. Repeat with the remaining 3 tortillas.

Parmesan ZUCCHINI CRISPS

CRAVING A CRISPY TASTE? These zucchini crisps give you crunch plus healthy vegetables. The best news: They take just minutes to make!

2 TABLESPOONS OLIVE OIL

1 CUP PANKO BREAD CRUMBS

1/2 CUP GRATED PARMESAN CHEESE

1/4 CUP MINCED FRESH CHIVES (OPTIONAL)

1/2 CUP ALL-PURPOSE FLOUR

1/2 TEASPOON KOSHER SALT

1/4 TEASPOON PEPPER

2 ZUCCHINI, SLICED INTO ROUNDS ABOUT 1/4 INCH THICK

2 LARGE EGGS, BEATEN

1. Warm the pan over medium heat, then add the oil.

2. In a large bowl, combine the panko, Parmesan, and chives (if using); set aside.

3. In a small bowl, combine the flour, salt, and pepper.

4. Working in batches, dredge each zucchini round in the flour mixture, dip into the eggs, then dredge in the panko mixture, pressing to coat.

5. Add the zucchini to the pan, and cook until evenly golden and crispy, about 1 minute on each side. Transfer to a plate lined with a paper towel.

Roasted
RED PEPPER DIP

THIS DIP IS SO DELICIOUS you would never guess it's healthy. Many versions use sour cream, but this recipe calls for Greek yogurt as a more nutritious (and just as tasty) substitution.

---

3 TABLESPOONS
OLIVE OIL, DIVIDED

2 MEDIUM RED BELL
PEPPERS, SEEDED AND
HALVED

1 CAN (15 OUNCES)
CHICKPEAS, DRAINED
AND RINSED

1/2 CUP GREEK YOGURT

2 CLOVES GARLIC

JUICE OF 1/2 LEMON

1/2 TEASPOON
GROUND CUMIN

KOSHER SALT TO TASTE

1. Warm the pan over medium heat, then add 1 tablespoon of the oil.

2. Brush the insides of the peppers with the remaining 2 tablespoons oil.

3. Add the peppers to the pan, cut-side down. Broil until charred, 8 to 10 minutes. Let cool; rub the skin off and finely chop the peppers.

4. In a food processor, blend the peppers with the chickpeas, Greek yogurt, garlic, lemon juice, cumin, and salt. Serve with fresh vegetables or pita chips.

Mozzarella EGGPLANT STACKS

EVEN THOSE WHO DON'T LOVE EGGPLANT will appreciate the fresh flavor in these appetizers. You can replace the shredded mozzarella with mozzarella slices for thicker, heartier stacks.

2 TEASPOONS PLUS
1 TABLESPOON OLIVE OIL,
DIVIDED

2 MEDIUM EGGPLANTS,
CUT INTO 12 ROUNDS
ABOUT 1/2 INCH THICK

1/2 TEASPOON
KOSHER SALT

1 CLOVE GARLIC, MINCED

2 LARGE TOMATOES,
EACH CUT INTO 3 SLICES
ABOUT 3/4 INCH THICK

1/2 CUP SHREDDED
MOZZARELLA CHEESE

FRESHLY GROUND
BLACK PEPPER

1. Warm the pan over medium heat, then add 1 tablespoon of the oil.

2. In a large bowl, toss the eggplant with the salt, garlic, and remaining 2 teaspoons olive oil. Sauté the eggplant for 5 minutes per side or until tender. Transfer to a large platter.

3. Place 6 eggplant rounds on a platter and layer with a slice of tomato and a sprinkle of mozzarella. Top with another eggplant round, and season with pepper to taste. Stick a toothpick in each for serving.

Asian Shrimp
LETTUCE WRAPS

SHRIMP MAKES A GREAT APPETIZER INGREDIENT because it cooks so quickly—especially when chopped, as in this recipe. Experiment with garnishes, such as chopped peanuts, scallions, and sesame seeds.

½ CUP REDUCED-SODIUM SOY SAUCE

¼ CUP FRESH LIME JUICE

4 TEASPOONS GRATED FRESH GINGER

2 TEASPOONS HONEY

2 CLOVES GARLIC, MINCED

1 CAN (8 OUNCES) SLICED WATER CHESTNUTS, DRAINED AND COARSELY CHOPPED

1 TABLESPOON OLIVE OIL

1 POUND RAW SHRIMP, PEELED, DEVEINED, AND CHOPPED INTO ½-INCH CHUNKS

1 HEAD BIBB OR BOSTON LETTUCE, LEAVES SEPARATED

1. In a small bowl, combine the soy sauce, lime juice, ginger, honey, and garlic.

2. Add the water chestnuts to the sauce. Stir to combine; set aside.

3. Warm the pan over medium heat, then add the oil. Add the shrimp in an even layer. Cook for 2 minutes, stirring often.

4. Add the sauce to the pan and stir well. Cook for 3 minutes, stirring often.

5. Remove the pan from the heat. Let the shrimp rest in the sauce for 2 minutes. Serve by spooning a few tablespoons of the shrimp mixture into the center of a lettuce leaf.

BEST BREAKFASTS AND BRUNCHES

Ham and Mushroom
PIZZA OMELET

OMELETS ARE CLASSIC ONE-PAN BREAKFASTS, but don't be afraid to wake up the presentation. Simply saving flavorful tomato slices as toppers gives your omelet a layered look and keeps your eggs from getting runny.

---

6 EGGS

2 TABLESPOONS ALL-PURPOSE FLOUR

1 TEASPOON DRIED OREGANO

1/2 TEASPOON GROUND CAYENNE

KOSHER SALT AND FRESHLY GROUND BLACK PEPPER

1 CUP CREAM

1 TABLESPOON CLARIFIED BUTTER

2 CUPS SLICED MUSHROOMS

1/2 CUP CHOPPED HAM

1 ROMA TOMATO, SLICED

1/2 CUP SHREDDED MOZZARELLA CHEESE

1/4 CUP CHOPPED FRESH DILL, FOR GARNISH

1/4 CUP CHOPPED FRESH PARSLEY, FOR GARNISH

1. In a large bowl, whisk together the eggs, flour, oregano, cayenne, salt, and pepper. Whisk in the cream.

2. Warm the pan over medium heat, then add the butter. Add the mushrooms and ham; cook for 8 minutes or until the mushrooms release their liquid and start to brown.

3. Pour in the egg mixture. Cook, stirring gently with a heatproof spatula, for about 2 minutes or until the eggs are about half set. Then cook without stirring until the eggs are set.

4. Arrange the tomato slices on top and sprinkle with mozzarella; cover the pan for 1 minute or until the cheese is melted. Garnish with dill and parsley.

Sweet Potato and
SAUSAGE FRITTATA

FAVORITE COMFORT-FOOD FLAVORS come together for a fabulous frittata that's company-worthy but simple enough to enjoy any busy day of the week. The Simply Ming Stovetop Oven makes cleanup super fast.

---

1 LARGE SWEET POTATO, PEELED AND CUT INTO 1/2-INCH PIECES

1 TABLESPOON CHILE OIL

1/2 POUND SPICY SAUSAGES, CASINGS REMOVED

1 LARGE YELLOW ONION, DICED

6 SCALLIONS, THINLY SLICED, WHITE AND GREEN SEPARATED

8 EGGS

1/2 CUP HEAVY CREAM

1 CUP SHREDDED SHARP CHEDDAR CHEESE

KOSHER SALT AND FRESHLY GROUND BLACK PEPPER

---

1. Place the sweet potato in a microwavable bowl; cover. Microwave on HIGH for 3 minutes or until tender, stirring once halfway. Set aside.

2. Warm the pan over medium heat, then add the oil. Add the sausage and cook for 3 minutes, breaking it up and stirring occasionally. Add the onion; cook for 2 minutes or until the onion is tender and the sausage is crumbled and no longer pink.

3. Add the sweet potato and scallion whites to the sausage mixture; stir to combine.

4. In a large bowl, whisk together the eggs and cream.

5. Pour the egg mixture over the sausage mixture. Cover the pan and reduce the heat to medium-low. Cook for 10 to 12 minutes or until set. Sprinkle with the Cheddar, and top with the scallion greens. Season with salt and pepper to taste.

Breakfast
STUFFED PEPPERS

PEPPERS ARE PERFECT FOR STUFFING with much more than just rice and meat. And you don't need to even turn on your oven to get baked flavor. Use your pan's rack insert to keep this savory breakfast on the stovetop.

---

4 LARGE RED BELL PEPPERS

8 EGGS

1/2 CUP SHREDDED CHEDDAR CHEESE

2 TABLESPOONS CHOPPED FRESH CHIVES

1/4 TEASPOON KOSHER SALT

1/4 TEASPOON FRESHLY GROUND BLACK PEPPER

1. Insert the rack for the pan, and warm the pan to medium heat, about 350°F.

2. Cut ½ inch off the stem end and seed each pepper. Carefully place the peppers on the pan rack cut-side up.

3. In a medium bowl, whisk together the eggs, Cheddar, chives, salt, and pepper.

4. Carefully pour the egg mixture into the peppers, filling each pepper about three-fourths full. Close the lid and cook until the peppers are tender and the egg mixture is set and slightly puffed, 25 to 30 minutes.

Very Berry PUFF PANCAKE

WITH INGREDIENTS YOU PROBABLY HAVE ON HAND, you can make an impressive breakfast that tastes like dessert. It's easy to switch up your berry choices for whatever is in season or the fruit you prefer.

4 LARGE EGGS

1 CUP WHOLE MILK

1 CUP ALL-PURPOSE FLOUR

¼ CUP SUGAR

½ TEASPOON LEMON ZEST

¼ TEASPOON KOSHER SALT

2 TABLESPOONS CLARIFIED BUTTER

1 CUP BLUEBERRIES

POWDERED SUGAR, SYRUP, OR FRESHLY WHIPPED CREAM, FOR TOPPING

1. Combine the eggs, milk, flour, sugar, lemon zest, and salt in a bowl; set aside.

2. Warm the pan over medium heat to about 400°F, then add the butter. Pour in the egg mixture, scatter the berries on top, and cover. Cook until puffed and cooked through, about 20 minutes.

3. Slice and serve, topped with powdered sugar, syrup, or freshly whipped cream.

Dark Chocolate— MAPLE QUINOA

EXPAND YOUR QUINOA WORLD when you introduce the grain to the rich flavors of maple and dark chocolate. It's nutritious enough to start your morning but luscious enough to enjoy as a treat later in the day as well.

1 CUP UNSWEETENED ALMOND MILK

1 CUP COCONUT MILK

1/8 TEASPOON KOSHER SALT

1 CUP QUINOA, RINSED

2 TABLESPOONS UNSWEETENED COCOA POWDER

2 TABLESPOONS PURE MAPLE SYRUP

1/4 TEASPOON GROUND CINNAMON

2 SQUARES DARK CHOCOLATE, GRATED

1. In the pan over medium heat, add the almond milk, coconut milk, and salt. Bring to a boil.

2. Add the quinoa and cocoa powder. Cover and reduce the heat to low. Simmer for 15 to 20 minutes, stirring occasionally, until the quinoa is tender and the liquid is absorbed.

3. Remove from the heat, and stir in the maple syrup and cinnamon. Top with the grated chocolate.

Almond Butter
STUFFED FRENCH TOAST

ANY KIND OF FRENCH TOAST IS A TREAT, but a double-decker helping held together by almond butter takes this morning favorite to a new level. Not a nut fan? Simply substitute your favorite jelly. You can even try a mixture of almond butter and jelly for a PB&J twist.

4 LARGE EGGS

1¼ CUPS MILK

1¼ TEASPOONS GROUND CINNAMON

¼ TEASPOON GROUND NUTMEG

1 TEASPOON VANILLA EXTRACT

PINCH OF KOSHER SALT

¾ CUP ALMOND BUTTER

12 THICK SLICES BREAD

½ TABLESPOON CLARIFIED BUTTER

SYRUP, POWDERED SUGAR, OR FRUIT, FOR TOPPING

1. In a large shallow dish, whisk together the eggs, milk, cinnamon, nutmeg, vanilla, and salt.

2. Spread 2 tablespoons of almond butter on each of 6 bread slices. Top with the remaining 6 bread slices and press around the edges to seal.

3. Warm the pan over medium heat, then melt the butter.

4. Dip the sandwiches into the egg mixture for a few seconds on each side. Cook the sandwiches until golden brown, 2 to 3 minutes per side. Top with maple syrup, powdered sugar, or fruit.

FRENCH TOAST STICKS
with Apple Dip

YOUR WHOLE FAMILY WILL LOVE the fun and flavor of dipping French toast sticks. Plan for a busy morning by making the dip ahead of time and storing in the fridge until you're ready to rewarm. Leftover dip? It's also delicious served with pita chips.

APPLE DIP

2 CUPS DICED APPLES

2 TABLESPOONS
LEMON JUICE

2 TABLESPOONS
BROWN SUGAR

1/4 TEASPOON
GROUND CINNAMON

1 TEASPOON CORNSTARCH
DISSOLVED IN
1 TEASPOON WATER

TOAST STICKS

1 1/2 CUPS MILK

4 EGGS

1 TABLESPOON
VANILLA EXTRACT

1 TEASPOON
GROUND CINNAMON

1/2 TEASPOON
KOSHER SALT

2 TABLESPOONS
APPLE BUTTER

1/2 TABLESPOON
CLARIFIED BUTTER

8 THICK SLICES BREAD,
CUT INTO 1-INCH STRIPS

1. To make the apple dip: In a small pan, combine the apples, lemon juice, brown sugar, and cinnamon. Bring to a boil over medium heat; continue cooking until the juice is extracted from the apples. Add the cornstarch mixture. Return to a boil; continue cooking until the sauce thickens. Set aside.

2. To make the toast sticks: In a medium bowl, whisk together the milk, eggs, vanilla, cinnamon, and salt. Whisk in the apple butter.

3. Warm the pan over medium heat, then melt the butter.

4. Dip the bread strips into the egg mixture. Then cook until golden brown, 2 to 3 minutes per side. Serve with the apple dip.

Egg and Chorizo
BREAKFAST BURRITO

A BREAKFAST BURRITO IS GREAT ON THE GO. With fiber-filled vegetables such as tomatoes and red bell pepper and protein from eggs and chorizo, this burrito will keep you fueled all morning long. Because the Simply Ming Stovetop Oven wipes clean so easily, you can use that same pan to warm the tortillas.

SALSA

8 ROMA TOMATOES, CHOPPED

1 LARGE RED BELL PEPPER, CHOPPED

1/4 MEDIUM RED ONION, CHOPPED

1/2 CUP FRESH CILANTRO

ZEST AND JUICE OF 1 LIME

1/8 TEASPOON GROUND CAYENNE

2 CLOVES GARLIC, MINCED

1 TEASPOON GROUND CUMIN

KOSHER SALT AND FRESHLY GROUND BLACK PEPPER

BURRITOS

2 TEASPOONS CORN OIL

8 OUNCES CHORIZO, CASINGS REMOVED

1 CUP PREPARED HASH BROWNS

8 LARGE EGGS

KOSHER SALT AND FRESHLY GROUND BLACK PEPPER

4 LARGE BURRITO-SIZE TORTILLAS

1/2 CUP FINELY SHREDDED MEXICAN BLEND CHEESE

1. To make the salsa: In the work bowl of a food processor, combine the tomatoes, pepper, and onion. Pulse until the desired consistency. Add the cilantro, lime zest and juice, cayenne, garlic, and cumin. Pulse to combine. Season with salt and pepper to taste.

2. To make the burritos: Warm the pan over medium heat, then add the oil. Add the chorizo and cook, breaking it up, until it is slightly crisp, about 5 minutes. Remove to a paper towel–lined plate using a slotted spoon. Add the hash browns to the pan and cook, stirring occasionally, until the potatoes are golden brown and crisp, 8 to 10 minutes.

3. In a medium bowl, whisk the eggs until frothy. Season with salt and pepper. Pour the eggs over the hash browns and cook, stirring, until the eggs are fluffy and just set, about 3 minutes. Remove from the pan and keep warm. Wipe out the pan, return it to the heat, and warm the tortillas one at a time in the pan.

4. On each tortilla, layer the egg mixture, chorizo, salsa, and cheese. Fold in the two sides and roll up tightly.

Simple SHAKSHOUKA

IF YOU HAVEN'T HAD THE PLEASURE, let us introduce you to shakshouka (also sometimes spelled shakshuka). It's a vegetarian one-dish meal that originates in North African and is now popular throughout the Middle East. Bring it home to your kitchen for a delicious, satisfying meal.

---

1 TABLESPOON CHILE OIL

1/2 LARGE ONION, CHOPPED

2 TABLESPOONS TOMATO PASTE

1 TEASPOON GROUND CUMIN

1 CLOVE GARLIC, MINCED

1 TEASPOON PAPRIKA

1/4 TEASPOON GROUND CAYENNE

2 JARRED ROASTED RED PEPPERS, CHOPPED

1 CAN (28 OUNCES) DICED TOMATOES (INCLUDING JUICE)

8 LARGE EGGS

KOSHER SALT AND FRESHLY GROUND BLACK PEPPER

1. Preheat the oven to 400°F. Warm the pan over medium heat, then add the oil. Add the onion and cook until softened, 5 to 8 minutes.

2. Add the tomato paste and cook until it darkens slightly, about 2 minutes. Stir in the cumin, garlic, paprika, and cayenne, and cook for about 30 seconds. Add the red peppers and tomatoes with juice. Simmer for about 2 minutes.

3. Using the back of a spoon, make 8 indentations in the tomato sauce and crack 1 egg into each. Transfer the pan to the oven and bake until the egg whites are set but the yolks are still soft, 5 to 8 minutes. Season with salt and pepper to taste.

Apple-Cinnamon BREAKFAST BOWL

OATMEAL OFTEN GETS AN UNFAIR SHAKE for being basic and bland. But we know it's smart for our health, as it's filled with fiber. The solution: fruit and just the right spices that sweeten the deal without sacrificing the health benefits.

1/2 TABLESPOON CLARIFIED BUTTER

1 MEDIUM APPLE, DICED

3 TABLESPOONS HONEY

1 TEASPOON GROUND CINNAMON

1/4 TEASPOON GROUND GINGER

1/4 TEASPOON GROUND NUTMEG

PINCH OF KOSHER SALT

2 CUPS WATER

1 CUP OLD-FASHIONED OATS

1/2 CUP CHOPPED WALNUTS

1. Warm the pan over medium heat, then melt the butter. Add the apples, honey, cinnamon, ginger, nutmeg, and salt. Cook for 3 minutes or until the apples soften.

2. Pour in the water and bring to a low boil. Add the oats and reduce the heat to low. Cook, stirring occasionally, for 3 to 5 minutes.

3. Add the walnuts and cook until most of the liquid is absorbed.

Bacon and Tomato AVOCADO TOAST

ALSO SOMETIMES CALLED BAT (Bacon, Avocado, and Tomato) toast, this version steps it up with chives and melted mozzarella cheese as the top layer.

4 SLICES CRUSTY ITALIAN BREAD

1/4 CUP EXTRA-VIRGIN OLIVE OIL

2 AVOCADOS, PEELED

2 TABLESPOONS MINCED FRESH CHIVES

2 TABLESPOONS MINCED FRESH PARSLEY

2 TEASPOONS LEMON JUICE

KOSHER SALT AND FRESHLY GROUND BLACK PEPPER

1 LARGE TOMATO, SLICED

4 SLICES COOKED BACON

4 SLICES MOZZARELLA CHEESE

1. Insert the rack for the pan. Warm the pan to medium heat, about 350°F.

2. Drizzle both sides of the bread slices with the olive oil. Place the bread on the rack and grill until golden brown, 2 to 3 minutes per side. Remove from the heat.

3. In a small bowl, mash the avocados with the chives, parsley, lemon juice, and salt and pepper to taste.

4. Spread each slice of bread with the avocado mixture, then layer with a slice of tomato, bacon, and mozzarella. Return the toast to the grill rack and cover the pan with the lid. Cook over low heat until the cheese is melted.

Zesty BREAKFAST POTATOES

CRISPY, SEASONED POTATOES are the perfect complement to any hot breakfast. Your Simply Ming Stovetop Oven helps conduct heat evenly, bringing golden goodness to every potato.

---

2 POUNDS POTATOES, PEELED AND DICED

1 TABLESPOON CHILE OIL

1 SHALLOT, MINCED

2 JALAPEÑO PEPPERS, MINCED

1/4 TEASPOON KOSHER SALT

1/4 TEASPOON FRESHLY GROUND BLACK PEPPER

1 CUP DICED HAM

2 CLOVES GARLIC, MINCED

FRESH PARSLEY, FOR GARNISH

1. In a large pot, bring water to a boil. Add the potatoes and cook for 5 minutes. Rinse under cold water; set aside.

2. Warm the pan over medium heat, then add the oil. Add the shallot and jalapeños, and cook for 5 minutes. Add the potatoes, spreading them out into an even layer. Season with the salt and pepper. Cook for 15 to 20 minutes, stirring halfway through. When golden and crispy, add the ham and cook for 5 minutes. Add the garlic and cook for 1 to 2 more minutes. Garnish with parsley.

Garden
VEGETABLE FRITTATA

FRITTATAS ARE A DELICIOUS WAY to frontload your day with vegetables. This dish features classic garden veggies, but feel free to swap in or out according to your taste preference. Whatever ingredients you choose, the Simply Ming Stovetop Oven cooks them perfectly.

1 TABLESPOON CLARIFIED BUTTER

1 CUP BROCCOLI FLORETS, STEAMED

1 RED BELL PEPPER, DICED

1 CUP FRESH SPINACH

8 EGGS

1/4 CUP MILK

1/2 CUP SHREDDED CHEDDAR CHEESE

8 CHERRY TOMATOES, HALVED

1. Preheat the oven to 350°F.

2. Warm the pan over medium heat, then add the butter. Add the broccoli, pepper, and spinach, and cook until just soft.

3. Meanwhile, in a large bowl, whisk together the eggs and milk. Stir in the Cheddar.

4. Remove the pan from the heat, and pour the egg mixture over the vegetables. Top with the cherry tomatoes. Bake for 15 to 20 minutes or until set.

SWEET POTATO HASH
with Egg and Spinach

THE INGREDIENTS ARE SIMPLE, but the taste is anything but when sautéed sweet potatoes, fresh spinach, and soft eggs come together. Bonus: With the Simply Ming Stovetop Oven, the dish goes from stovetop to oven with ease.

1 TABLESPOON CHILE OIL

4 MEDIUM SWEET POTATOES, PEELED AND CUT INTO ½-INCH CUBES

½ TEASPOON KOSHER SALT

½ TEASPOON FRESHLY GROUND BLACK PEPPER

½ TEASPOON GROUND CUMIN

2 CUPS PACKED FRESH SPINACH

6 EGGS

1. Preheat the oven to 425°F. Warm the pan over medium heat, then add the oil. Add the sweet potatoes, salt, pepper, and cumin. Cook for 10 to 15 minutes, stirring often, until browned and just tender.

2. Stir in the spinach. Cook for 3 minutes or until the spinach wilts. Remove from the heat.

3. Carefully crack the eggs over the top, spacing evenly apart. Transfer the pan to the oven and bake until the egg whites are set but the yolks are still soft, 5 to 8 minutes.

PUMPKIN CREPES
with Berry Jam

DO YOU CRAVE ALL THINGS PUMPKIN, especially in the fall? Here's a light twist on the pumpkin-flavor craze that comes together so easily in your Simply Ming Stovetop Oven.

2 EGGS

2 CUPS MILK, WARMED

2 TABLESPOONS
CLARIFIED BUTTER,
MELTED

1/2 CUP PUMPKIN PUREE

1 TEASPOON VANILLA
EXTRACT

1 1/2 CUPS FLOUR

1 TABLESPOON SUGAR

1/2 TEASPOON
BAKING POWDER

1/2 TEASPOON
KOSHER SALT

1 TEASPOON
GROUND CINNAMON

1/4 TEASPOON
GROUND GINGER

1/4 TEASPOON
GROUND NUTMEG

PINCH OF
GROUND CLOVES

1 TEASPOON
CLARIFIED BUTTER

BERRY JAM, FOR TOPPING

1. In a medium bowl, whisk together the eggs, milk, and melted butter. Mix in the pumpkin puree and vanilla.

2. In a large bowl, combine the flour, sugar, baking powder, salt, cinnamon, ginger, nutmeg, and cloves. Gradually mix the liquid mixture into the dry ingredients until smooth.

3. Warm the pan over medium heat, then melt the butter. Pour the batter into the pan 1/3 cup at a time, twirling the pan so the crepe batter thins and spreads out covering the pan. Flip when the top is almost set. Remove from the pan 30 seconds after flipping. Keep the crepes warm on a baking sheet in the oven. Repeat with the remaining batter. Serve the crepes topped with berry jam.

Black Bean
BREAKFAST SKILLET

YOU'LL FIND THIS DISH HEARTY enough to work for breakfast or dinner. If you're paring back on carbs, it makes a great choice because it's packed with flavor. Plus, with just six ingredients and using a pan that goes from stovetop to oven, it's super simple.

---

1 CAN (15 OUNCES) BLACK BEANS, DRAINED AND RINSED

1 CAN (14.5 OUNCES) ITALIAN-STYLE DICED TOMATOES

1 TEASPOON GROUND CUMIN

6 EGGS

¼ CUP SHREDDED CHEDDAR CHEESE

FRESH CILANTRO, FOR GARNISH

1. Preheat the oven to 425°F. Warm the pan over medium heat. Add the beans, tomatoes, and cumin. Cook for 8 to 10 minutes, until the tomato juice reduces. Remove from the heat.

2. Using the back of a spoon, make 6 indentations in the bean mixture and crack 1 egg into each. Transfer the pan to the oven and bake until the egg whites are set but the yolks are still soft, 5 to 8 minutes.

3. Remove from the oven and top with the Cheddar. Bake for 5 more minutes. Garnish with cilantro.

Thai SCRAMBLED EGGS

BORED OF BREAKFAST? MAKE IT AN ADVENTURE by trying internationally inspired dishes. A touch of coconut, chile pepper, and basil give the usual scrambled eggs Thai flair.

2 TEASPOONS COCONUT OIL

1 SERRANO PEPPER, SEEDED AND DICED

2 SPRING ONIONS, SLICED

6 LARGE EGGS

1 TABLESPOON COCONUT MILK

1/4 CUP CHOPPED TOMATO

12 ROUGHLY CHOPPED FRESH BASIL LEAVES

1. Warm the pan over medium heat, then add the coconut oil. Add the pepper and spring onions; cook for about 2 minutes.

2. Meanwhile, in a medium bowl, whisk together the eggs and coconut milk.

3. Pour the egg mixture into the pan, stirring with a spatula. Continue moving the eggs around until all are cooked. Stir in the basil.

FRIED EGG SANDWICH
with Spinach

FRIED EGG ON TOAST IS A CLASSIC. But adding fresh spinach and just the right seasoning can lend a little something extra without overwhelming. Your Simply Ming Stovetop Oven makes it convenient to try all sorts of new variations on the basic egg sandwich.

---

2 SLICES WHOLE-GRAIN BREAD

1 TEASPOON CLARIFIED BUTTER

2 EGGS

1/4 CUP FRESH BABY SPINACH

KOSHER SALT AND FRESHLY GROUND BLACK PEPPER

CHOPPED FRESH THYME, FOR GARNISH

1. Toast the bread slices; set aside.

2. Warm the pan over medium heat, then add the butter. Crack both eggs into the pan. Immediately reduce the heat to low. Cook slowly until the whites are completely set and the yolks begin to thicken but are still soft. Carefully flip each egg and cook on the other side to the desired doneness.

3. To serve open-face style, top each bread slice with spinach and an egg. Season with salt and pepper to taste. Garnish with thyme.

Homemade
SAGE SAUSAGE

SURE, YOU CAN BUY PRESEASONED SAUSAGE, but making your own is easier than you might think. And it gives you control over the ingredients—keep out preservatives and adjust the seasoning to your liking.

1 POUND LEAN GROUND PORK

1 TABLESPOON DRIED SAGE

1 TEASPOON KOSHER SALT

1 TEASPOON BROWN SUGAR

1/2 TEASPOON DRIED THYME

1/2 TEASPOON FRESHLY GROUND BLACK PEPPER

1/4 TEASPOON DRIED MARJORAM

1/8 TEASPOON RED PEPPER FLAKES

PINCH OF GROUND CLOVES

1. In a large bowl, combine the pork, sage, salt, sugar, thyme, black pepper, marjoram, pepper flakes, and cloves. Mix the ingredients with clean hands until well combined. Form the mixture into 8 patties.

2. Warm the pan over medium heat. Fry the patties for 3 to 4 minutes per side until browned and the meat is cooked through.

Creamy Sage
SAUSAGE GRAVY

SAUSAGE GRAVY ISN'T LIMITED to Southern enjoyment. Though it has its roots in the South, the creamy comfort is a breakfast treat for all when enjoyed atop a flaky biscuit or toasted bread.

1 POUND HOMEMADE SAGE SAUSAGE (PAGE 56)

2 TABLESPOONS CLARIFIED BUTTER

1/4 CUP ALL-PURPOSE FLOUR

3 CUPS WHOLE MILK

1/2 TEASPOON KOSHER SALT

1 TEASPOON FRESHLY GROUND BLACK PEPPER

1/4 TEASPOON DRIED THYME

1. Warm the pan over medium heat. Add the sausage, crumbling it as it browns. Add the butter and stir until well combined.

2. Reduce the heat to low and add the flour, stirring to combine. Cook for 2 to 3 minutes.

3. Pour in the milk, stirring frequently, until it thickens to your desired consistency, 5 to 10 minutes.

4. Remove from the heat, and stir in the salt, pepper, and thyme. Serve over biscuits, whole-grain toast, or bread of your choice.

AMAZING
MAINS

Coconut CHICKEN CURRY

THIS EASY CURRY IS A FAST, HEALTHY WAY to feed your family. Thigh meat will be richer and moister, but breast meat will please the white-meat lovers in your house. Try a mix of both if you can't decide on one or the other. This makes superb leftovers—even cold out of the fridge.

2 POUNDS BONELESS, SKINLESS CHICKEN BREASTS OR THIGHS (ABOUT 4 BREASTS OR 7 THIGHS), CUT INTO 1-INCH CUBES

2 1/2 TEASPOONS MILD CURRY POWDER

1 1/2 TEASPOONS KOSHER SALT

1 TEASPOON GROUND CUMIN

1 TEASPOON GROUND TURMERIC

1/2 TEASPOON FRESHLY GROUND BLACK PEPPER

1/8 TEASPOON GROUND CAYENNE

1/8 TEASPOON WHITE PEPPER

2 TABLESPOONS COCONUT OIL

1/2 MEDIUM ONION, CHOPPED

1 CUP CHOPPED RED BELL PEPPER

1 CAN (14 OUNCES) COCONUT MILK

1 PIECE (2 1/2 INCHES) FRESH GINGER, PEELED AND CHOPPED

4 CLOVES GARLIC, PEELED

5 OUNCES FRESH BABY SPINACH

1. In a medium bowl, toss the chicken with the curry powder, salt, cumin, turmeric, black pepper, cayenne, and white pepper.

2. Warm the pan over medium heat, then add the oil. Add the onion and pepper, and cook, stirring, until softened, about 2 minutes.

3. Puree the coconut milk, ginger, and garlic in a blender until very smooth.

4. Add the chicken and coconut milk mixture to the pan and cook, tossing occasionally, until the chicken is cooked through and the sauce has thickened, 7 to 10 minutes.

5. Fold the spinach into the chicken mixture and cook until wilted, about 1 minute. Serve over rice.

One-Pan
CHICKEN CACCIATORE

"HUNTER'S CHICKEN" IS A RUSTIC ITALIAN DISH made from the spoils of the hunt—fresh chicken (or rabbit), along with savory aromatics and a lush tomato-based sauce. It's a satisfying dish that freezes well.

4 CHICKEN THIGHS,
2 DRUMSTICKS, AND
2 CHICKEN BREASTS
(BONE-IN WITH SKIN)

1/4 CUP FLOUR

KOSHER SALT AND
FRESHLY GROUND
BLACK PEPPER

2 TABLESPOONS
OLIVE OIL

2 TABLESPOONS
CLARIFIED BUTTER

1 LARGE ONION, CHOPPED

1 LARGE RED BELL
PEPPER, CUT INTO STRIPS

1 CAN (28 OUNCES)
TOMATOES, CUT UP
AND JUICE RESERVED

1 CAN (8 OUNCES)
TOMATO SAUCE

1 CAN (6 OUNCES)
TOMATO PASTE

1 CUP DRY RED WINE
OR WATER

1/2 CUP CHOPPED
FRESH BASIL, PLUS
LEAVES FOR GARNISH

1 CUP MEDIUM
BLACK OLIVES, PITTED

1. Dredge the chicken in the flour, and season with salt and pepper.

2. Warm the pan over medium heat, then add the oil and butter. Add the chicken and brown on all sides. Remove the chicken to a platter.

3. Add the onion and pepper to the pan and cook for 5 minutes, until softened. Stir in the tomatoes, tomato sauce, tomato paste, wine, and basil. Bring to a boil and add the olives. Reduce the heat to low; cover, and simmer for 30 minutes.

4. Return the chicken to the pan. Cover and simmer for 45 to 60 minutes or until the chicken is tender. Garnish with fresh basil.

Ginger Braised WHOLE CHICKEN

THIS IS A SIMPLE AND SATISFYING HOMESTYLE MEAL that is just the thing to make when someone in your house has a cold! The pungent ginger and warm broth make this soup a healing, delicious treat, and it's so easy to make that you might find it in your regular weekly rotation.

3 RIBS CELERY, CUT INTO ½-INCH PIECES

2 LARGE CARROTS, PEELED AND CUT INTO ½-INCH PIECES

1 LARGE ONION, CHOPPED

1 TEASPOON BLACK PEPPERCORNS

2 BAY LEAVES

2 SPRIGS FRESH THYME

¼ BUNCH FRESH PARSLEY, CHOPPED

2 STAR ANISE

1 TABLESPOONS MINCED GINGER

¼ CUP REDUCED-SODIUM SOY SAUCE

1½ QUARTS REDUCED-SODIUM CHICKEN BROTH

KOSHER SALT AND FRESHLY GROUND BLACK PEPPER

1 WHOLE CHICKEN, 4 TO 5 POUNDS, WING TIPS FOLDED OVER THE BACK

1. In the pan, combine the celery, carrots, onion, peppercorns, bay leaves, thyme, parsley, star anise, ginger, and soy sauce. Add the stock and season with salt and pepper.

2. Season the chicken inside and out with salt and pepper. Add the chicken to the pan breast-side up. It should be completely covered with stock, but if not, add more.

3. Cover and bring just to a simmer over medium-high heat. Reduce the heat to low and barely simmer for 45 minutes. Turn off the heat and let the pan stand, covered, for 30 minutes to 1 hour (the chicken won't cook any more after 30 minutes). Discard the bay leaves, thyme sprigs, and star anise. Remove the chicken and strain the broth, reserving the vegetables. Carve the chicken and serve with the vegetables and bowls of the broth.

GINGER CHICKEN THIGHS
with Parsnips

MOST CHEFS WILL TELL YOU the thighs are their favorite part of the chicken—they're flavorful, moist, and easy to cook. And they're inexpensive, too! This recipe is a crowd-pleaser that's easy enough to make on weeknights and impressive enough for company.

---

2 POUNDS
CHICKEN THIGHS

KOSHER SALT AND
FRESHLY GROUND
BLACK PEPPER

3 TABLESPOONS
OLIVE OIL, DIVIDED

2 LARGE ONIONS,
DICED

2 TABLESPOONS
MINCED GINGER

3 LARGE PARSNIPS,
PEELED AND CUT INTO
1-INCH PIECES

4 RIBS CELERY, CUT
INTO 1-INCH PIECES

5 SPRIGS FRESH THYME

1. Preheat the oven to 450°F. Season the thighs with salt and pepper.

2. Warm the pan over medium heat, then add 2 tablespoons of the oil. When the oil is hot, add the thighs skin-side down. Brown, turning once, for about 10 minutes. Transfer the thighs to a platter.

3. Add the remaining 1 tablespoon oil to the pan, swirl, and heat. When the oil is hot, add the onions, ginger, parsnips, celery, and thyme. Season with salt and pepper. Cook the vegetables, stirring, until softened, about 6 minutes. Remove from the heat.

4. In the pan, add the thighs, skin-side up, on top of the vegetables. Bake uncovered until the vegetables are soft, the chicken is cooked through, and a thermometer inserted into the thickest part registers 165°F, 30 to 40 minutes.

Brined ROAST CHICKEN

BRINING IS THE SECRET TO MOIST, delicious roast chicken. During the brining process, the chicken absorbs the flavorful liquid, so even the white meat won't dry out in the oven. The little bit of sugar added to the brine helps the skin brown and crisp.

1/3 CUP KOSHER SALT FOR BRINING, PLUS MORE TO SEASON

1/3 CUP SUGAR

1 CHICKEN, 6 TO 8 POUNDS

3 TABLESPOONS OLIVE OIL, DIVIDED

2 TABLESPOONS MINCED GARLIC

2 TABLESPOONS MINCED FRESH THYME, DIVIDED

FRESHLY GROUND BLACK PEPPER

1 TABLESPOON MINCED GINGER

2 TABLESPOONS AGAVE SYRUP OR HONEY

3 LARGE SWEET POTATOES, PEELED AND CUT INTO 1-INCH PIECES

1 BUNCH SCALLIONS, WHITE AND GREEN PARTS THINLY SLICED

1. The day before, brine the chicken. In a large pitcher, combine the 1/3 cup salt and the sugar with 8 cups water, and stir until both dissolve. Put the chicken in a bowl or pot large enough to hold it and the brine, and pour the brine over the chicken. If the chicken isn't covered, make more brine and add it to the bowl. Refrigerate overnight. The next day, rinse the chicken and pat dry.

2. Preheat the oven to 500°F. Place the pan on the middle oven rack to heat.

3. Rub the chicken inside and out with 2 tablespoons of the olive oil, the garlic, and 1 tablespoon of the thyme. Season with salt and pepper inside and out.

4. In a large bowl, combine the ginger, syrup, sweet potatoes, scallions, the remaining 1 tablespoon thyme, and the remaining 1 tablespoon oil. Mix well and season with salt and pepper.

5. Pull out the oven rack with the pan and add the vegetables, which will sizzle. Top with the chicken, breast-side up, and roast for 15 minutes. Lower the oven temperature to 375°F and continue to roast, turning the pan once front to back and stirring the sweet potatoes halfway through cooking. Roast until the chicken is cooked through and a thermometer inserted into the thigh registers 165°F, about 1¼ hours longer. If the chicken is coloring too quickly, tent it with foil. Remove the tent and let the chicken cook for 10 minutes more so the skin crisps.

6. Transfer the chicken to a cutting board to rest for 10 minutes. Transfer the sweet potatoes to a platter. Carve the chicken and place on top of the sweet potatoes. Spoon the pan juices over the chicken to serve.

Smoked JERK CHICKEN

IF YOU WISH YOU WERE EATING AT A BEACH bar on the Caribbean right now (and who doesn't?), treat yourself to this mildly spicy, juicy jerk chicken. Just like the chicken you get at beach bars in Jamaica, this version is even easier, because it's smoked in your Simply Ming Stovetop Oven.

MARINADE
6 TABLESPOONS VEGETABLE OIL

2 TABLESPOONS MOLASSES

JUICE OF 1 LIME

2 JALAPEÑO PEPPERS, STEMMED AND SEEDED

½ TABLESPOON MINCED GINGER

1 TABLESPOON MINCED FRESH THYME

1½ TEASPOONS ALLSPICE

1 TEASPOON ONION POWDER

1 TEASPOON GARLIC POWDER

1 TEASPOON KOSHER SALT

¼ TEASPOON PEPPER

3 POUNDS CHICKEN THIGHS, DRUMSTICKS, AND/OR BREASTS (BONE-IN WITH SKIN)

1. To make the marinade: In the work bowl of a food processor, combine the oil, molasses, lime juice, peppers, ginger, thyme, allspice, onion power, garlic powder, salt, and pepper. Pulse until combined. Set aside ¼ cup of the marinade.

2. In a large ziplock bag, add the chicken and pour in the marinade. Marinate in the refrigerator for at least an hour or preferably overnight.

3. Line the bottom of the pan with aluminum foil. Place 1 tablespoon of stovetop wood chips on the foil, and warm the pan over medium heat. Place the rack insert in the pan. When the chips start smoking, remove the chicken from the marinade and place it on the rack. Cover and cook for 15 minutes. Turn the burner off and let the chicken sit covered for 15 more minutes. Transfer the chicken to a platter, and remove the rack and foil from the pan.

4. Preheat the oven to 350°F. Transfer the chicken back to the pan. Put the pan in the oven and cook for 45 minutes or until a thermometer inserted into thickest part reaches 165°F.

5. Remove the pan from the oven and brush the chicken with the reserved marinade. Return the pan to the oven and broil for 3 to 4 minutes or until the skin is brown and crispy.

New Orleans Style CHICKEN AND SAUSAGE GUMBO

A GOOD CREOLE GUMBO IS ALL ABOUT THE ROUX—the fat and flour mixture that thickens the stew. It's important not to rush this step and to cook the roux over low heat until it is dark brown and fragrant. Andouille is spicy, so if you prefer a milder sausage, use the kielbasa.

2 CUPS SLICED VIDALIA ONIONS

1 PACKAGE (10 OUNCES) FROZEN CUT OKRA, THAWED

1 LARGE GREEN BELL PEPPER, SEEDED AND CHOPPED

4 RIBS CELERY WITH LEAVES, SLICED

3/4 CUP FINELY CHOPPED FRESH PARSLEY, DIVIDED

5 CLOVES GARLIC, THINLY SLICED

2 BAY LEAVES

2 TEASPOONS SALT

1 TEASPOON DRIED THYME

1 TEASPOON GROUND CAYENNE

1 TEASPOON FRESHLY GROUND BLACK PEPPER

1 TABLESPOON PLUS 1/3 CUP VEGETABLE OIL, DIVIDED

12 CHICKEN THIGHS

1 POUND COOKED ANDOUILLE SAUSAGE OR KIELBASA, SLICED 1/2 INCH THICK

2/3 CUP FLOUR

6 CUPS REDUCED-SODIUM CHICKEN BROTH

1 CAN (6 OUNCES) TOMATO PASTE

2 CUPS WATER

1 CAN (14 TO 16 OUNCES) WHOLE PEELED TOMATOES, DRAINED AND CHOPPED

1/2 SCALLION, CHOPPED

2 TABLESPOONS DISTILLED WHITE VINEGAR, OR TO TASTE

1. In a large bowl, combine the onions, okra, bell pepper, celery, 1/4 cup of the parsley, garlic, bay leaves, salt, thyme, cayenne, and black pepper. Set aside.

2. Warm the pan over medium heat, then add 1 tablespoon of the oil. Add the chicken, cooking in batches, until browned, about 5 minutes per side. Transfer to a large bowl.

3. Add the sausage to the pan over medium heat, stirring constantly. Cook until lightly browned, about 6 minutes. Transfer to the bowl with the chicken.

4. Pour the fat from the pan into a glass measuring cup and add enough of the remaining ⅓ cup vegetable oil to equal ⅔ cup. Transfer the fat mixture back to the pan and warm over medium-low heat, scraping up any browned bits. Slowly whisk in the flour and cook, stirring frequently, until it is a very dark, rich brown, about 30 minutes.

5. Add the broth and again scrape up any browned bits.

6. In another bowl, blend the tomato paste with the 2 cups water. Stir the mixture into the broth. Add the tomatoes, reserved vegetables, chicken, and sausage. Bring to a boil over high heat; reduce the heat to low and simmer for 1 hour until thickened.

7. Stir in the remaining ½ cup parsley, scallions, and vinegar. Cook, stirring, for 5 minutes. Remove from the heat, cover, and let stand for 10 minutes. Discard the bay leaves. Serve with rice.

Roasted
CHICKEN PROVENÇAL

THE FLAVORS OF PROVENCE ARE EASY to recreate in this simple roast chicken recipe. You can find herbes de Provence at any supermarket, and they are the secret ingredient that makes this chicken recipe special. They are also great on roasted potatoes or grilled vegetables.

2 CLOVES GARLIC, FINELY CHOPPED

1/4 CUP HERBES DE PROVENCE

1 TABLESPOON CHOPPED FRESH THYME

1/4 CUP OLIVE OIL

1 TABLESPOON KOSHER SALT

1/2 TEASPOON FRESHLY GROUND BLACK PEPPER

1 CHICKEN, 3 1/2 TO 4 POUNDS

1. Preheat the oven to 475°F. Insert the rack for the pan.

2. In a small bowl, combine the garlic, herbes de Provence, thyme, oil, salt, and pepper. Rub the mixture on the inside and outside of the chicken. Place the chicken on the rack set inside the pan.

3. Roast the chicken uncovered until the skin begins to brown, 25 to 30 minutes. Reduce the heat to 350°F, and cook until a thermometer inserted into a thigh registers 165°F, 25 to 30 minutes. Let the chicken rest for 10 minutes before carving.

One-Pan CHICKEN ALFREDO PASTA

A CREAMY, COMFORTING PASTA DISH with the rich flavor of Parmesan cheese, this recipe is as impressive as it is easy. Think of it as a grown-up version of macaroni and cheese!

---

2 POUNDS SKINLESS, BONELESS CHICKEN BREASTS, CUT INTO 1-INCH PIECES

KOSHER SALT AND FRESHLY GROUND BLACK PEPPER

2 TABLESPOONS CLARIFIED BUTTER

1/2 TEASPOON GROUND NUTMEG

1 TEASPOON MINCED GARLIC

4 CUPS REDUCED-SODIUM CHICKEN BROTH

1 POUND PENNE RIGATE OR ZITI

1 1/2 CUPS HEAVY CREAM, WARMED

1 CUP GRATED PARMESAN CHEESE, PLUS MORE FOR SERVING

1/4 CUP CHOPPED FRESH PARSLEY (OPTIONAL)

1. Season the chicken with salt and pepper.

2. Warm the pan over medium-high heat, then add the butter. Add the chicken, in batches if necessary, and cook until browned, about 4 minutes. Remove the chicken to a plate; leave any browned bits in the pan. Sprinkle the nutmeg on the chicken.

3. Reduce the heat to medium, and add the garlic to the pan. Cook for about 30 seconds, until fragrant. Increase the heat to high, add the chicken broth, and scrape up the browned bits on the bottom of the pan. Lower to medium heat, and simmer for 5 minutes.

4. Stir in the pasta and continue simmering until the pasta is just starting to soften, about 8 minutes. Stir in the warm heavy cream. Add the chicken and any accumulated juices. Cover and simmer, stirring occasionally, until the pasta is tender, most of the liquid has been absorbed, and the chicken is cooked through, about 4 minutes more. Remove from the heat, and stir in the Parmesan and parsley (if using).

5. Serve with additional Parmesan.

ROAST TURKEY BREAST
Porchetta Style

PORCHETTA IS A FAVORITE ITALIAN ROAST PORK that involves fennel and pancetta, and this version swaps out the traditional pork loin for turkey breast, which is easier to find. This savory recipe is a great way to add strong flavor to an otherwise mild meat. If you want it more or less spicy, feel free to adjust the amount of red pepper flakes.

---

2 TABLESPOONS OLIVE OIL

2 OUNCES PANCETTA, CHOPPED

4 CLOVES GARLIC

1/2 CUP CHOPPED PARSLEY

1/4 CUP COARSELY CHOPPED FRESH CHIVES

1 TEASPOON FINELY CHOPPED FRESH ROSEMARY

1 TEASPOON CHOPPED FRESH OREGANO

2 TEASPOONS FINELY GRATED LEMON ZEST

1 TEASPOON GROUND FENNEL SEEDS

1/2 TEASPOON RED PEPPER FLAKES

1 TABLESPOON KOSHER SALT

1 WHOLE TURKEY BREAST, SKIN ON, BONELESS

12 SLICES BACON

1. Preheat the oven to 325°F.

2. Warm the pan over medium heat, then add the oil. Add the pancetta. Cook, stirring, until brown and crisp, 5 to 8 minutes. Let cool. Transfer the pancetta and fat in the pan to a food processor. Add the garlic, and process to a smooth paste. Add the parsley, chives, rosemary, oregano, and lemon zest. Process until smooth. Set aside.

3. In a small bowl, combine the fennel, red pepper flakes, and salt. Set aside.

4. Pat the turkey breast dry and place it skin-side up on a cutting board. Working with one fillet of the breast at a time, run your fingers and a knife under the skin to remove it. Turn the breast over, skin-side down, flat on a cutting board. Using a thin, sharp

knife, cut each fillet parallel to the board, a bit more than halfway across. Lift back the resulting flap. It should resemble an open book. This is called butterflying the breast. Do the same with the other fillet.

5. Pat the turkey dry and place skin-side down in the pan. Run your fingers underneath the fillets lengthwise to detach. Using a thin, sharp blade, position the knife about 3 inches from the neck end and cut downward at a 45-degree angle into the thickest part of the breast (do not cut all the way through; you're butterflying only the top portion). Open the top flap you've just created like a book.

6. Fold the fillets in half and place in the top and bottom gaps between the breasts so the tapered ends are facing in. The idea is to create a layer of meat of uniform thickness across the entire breast.

7. Rub the garlic paste over the inside and outside of the turkey. Do the same with the spice mixture.

8. Roll up the turkey breast, left to right, like a jelly roll, to form a log. Place it seam-side down and tuck the skin under at each end. Starting at the center, tie the breast with kitchen twine at even intervals (apply some pressure with the string so the turkey holds a nice round shape, but don't tie it too tightly or it will bulge when cooked). Let the rolled turkey sit for 2 hours to bring to room temperature.

9. Roast the turkey until golden and starting to crisp, 40 to 45 minutes. Remove from the oven and carefully remove the strings with kitchen shears. Drape with the bacon, overlapping; tuck the ends underneath the turkey to secure. Roast until a thermometer inserted into the thickest part registers 140°F, 30 to 40 minutes. Increase the oven temperature to 400°F and cook until the bacon is browned and crisp and the thermometer registers 150°F, 5 to 10 minutes. Transfer to a platter and let rest for at least 40 minutes before slicing. Serve with the pan juices.

Easy Chicken
TORTILLA SOUP

THIS SOUP IS EASY TO MAKE with a store-bought rotisserie chicken, so feel free to skip the step of cooking your own. It freezes very well, and it's great to have a secret stash of dinners in the freezer for those busy nights when you just don't feel like cooking.

TORTILLA STRIPS
10 SMALL CORN TORTILLAS, CUT INTO 1/4-INCH-WIDE STRIPS

2 TABLESPOONS OLIVE OIL

1 TEASPOON KOSHER SALT, OR TO TASTE

SOUP
2 TABLESPOONS OLIVE OIL

1 CUP DICED VIDALIA OR YELLOW ONION (ABOUT 1 MEDIUM ONION)

1 LARGE JALAPEÑO PEPPER (4 TO 5 INCHES LONG), SEEDED AND DICED

3 CLOVES GARLIC, FINELY MINCED

32 OUNCES REDUCED-SODIUM CHICKEN BROTH

2 CANS (14.5 OUNCES) DICED TOMATOES, WITH JUICE

1 CAN (15 OUNCES) BLACK BEANS, DRAINED AND RINSED

2 CUPS SHREDDED COOKED CHICKEN

1 TABLESPOON LIME JUICE

1 TABLESPOON CHILI POWDER

2 TEASPOONS GROUND CUMIN

2 TEASPOONS KOSHER SALT, OR TO TASTE

1 TEASPOON FRESHLY GROUND BLACK PEPPER

1 TEASPOON SMOKED PAPRIKA

1/4 TEASPOON GROUND CAYENNE, OR TO TASTE (OPTIONAL)

1/3 CUP FINELY MINCED FRESH CILANTRO

DICED AVOCADO, FOR SERVING (OPTIONAL)

SHREDDED MONTEREY JACK CHEESE, FOR SERVING (OPTIONAL)

SOUR CREAM, FOR SERVING (OPTIONAL)

1. To make the tortilla strips: Preheat the oven to 375°F. On a baking sheet lined with foil, scatter the tortilla strips, drizzle with the oil, and season with the kosher salt. Toss to evenly coat. Bake for about 15 minutes or until crisp and lightly golden brown; set aside.

2. To make the soup: Warm the pan over medium-high heat, then add the oil. Add the onion and jalapeño. Sauté for about 5 minutes until the vegetables begin to soften, stirring occasionally. Add the garlic and sauté for 1 to 2 minutes. Add the chicken broth, tomatoes and juice, black beans, chicken, lime juice, chili powder, cumin, salt, pepper, paprika, and cayenne (if using). Bring to a boil; continue to boil gently 5 to 7 minutes. Add 1 to 2 cups of water at any time, for preferred consistency. Add the cilantro and boil for 1 minute. Add more salt, pepper, or other seasonings to taste.

3. Ladle the soup into bowls. Top with the tortilla strips. Garnish with avocado, cheese, or sour cream, if desired.

GREEK EGG AND LEMON SOUP *with Orzo*

SAVOR A DELICIOUS CHICKEN SOUP that combines the bright flavor of lemon with a rich chicken stock and hearty orzo for a one-pot meal that's perfect for a chilly evening. The eggs add a unique body to the stock, and you can use rice if you don't have orzo.

1 WHOLE CHICKEN, ABOUT 3½ POUNDS, WITH EXCESS FAT TRIMMED AND BREAST SKIN REMOVED

2 CARROTS, PEELED AND HALVED

2 RIBS CELERY, HALVED

1 LARGE ONION, HALVED

2 BAY LEAVES

5 WHOLE BLACK PEPPERCORNS

2 TEASPOONS SALT PLUS MORE FOR SEASONING, TO TASTE

12 CUPS WATER

½ CUP ORZO PASTA

3 EGGS, AT ROOM TEMPERATURE

1 TEASPOON LEMON ZEST

JUICE OF 2 LEMONS

KOSHER SALT AND FRESHLY GROUND BLACK PEPPER

CHOPPED FRESH PARSLEY, FOR GARNISH

CHOPPED SCALLIONS, FOR GARNISH

1. Warm the pan over medium-high heat, then add the chicken, carrots, celery, onion, bay leaves, peppercorns, salt, and water. Bring to a rapid boil, then decrease the heat to medium-low and simmer, partially covered, for 1 to 1½ hours.

2. Transfer the chicken and vegetables to a bowl. Strain the broth through a fine sieve into a separate large bowl. Return the strained broth to the pan and bring to a boil.

3. Pull the chicken off the bones and add the chicken and vegetables to the broth. Add the orzo and cook, uncovered, for 10 to 12 minutes until tender. Remove from the heat.

4. In a medium bowl, whisk the eggs until frothy. Add the lemon zest and juice while continuing to whisk.

5. When the orzo is cooked, slowly add 2 cups of the hot broth to the egg-lemon mixture while continuing to whisk, to temper the eggs and prevent curdling.

6. Add the egg-lemon mixture to the pan and warm over very low heat for 5 to 10 minutes until heated through (never boiling). Discard the bay leaves. Season with salt and pepper to taste. Garnish with parsley and scallions.

RED ROAST DUCK LEGS
with Sweet Potatoes and Daikon

MOST PEOPLE THINK DUCK is just for restaurants, but it's deceptively easy to cook at home. This recipe is a great way to start, because the braising technique is very forgiving—you can't overcook these duck legs! And the spicy, fragrant liquid is irresistible over rice.

BRAISING SAUCE

4 CUPS REDUCED-SODIUM SOY SAUCE

2 CUPS RED WINE

2 POUNDS ROCK SUGAR

1 PIECE (3 INCHES) GINGER, CUT INTO 1/4-INCH SLICES

3 DRIED THAI BIRD CHILES

1 MEDIUM HEAD GARLIC, HALVED HORIZONTALLY

1 STAR ANISE

1 BUNCH SCALLIONS, WHITE AND GREEN PARTS CUT INTO 3-INCH LENGTHS

1 MEDIUM UNPEELED ORANGE, WASHED AND QUARTERED

2 CINNAMON STICKS

DUCK AND POTATOES

10 DUCK LEGS (LEGS WITH THIGHS)

1 LARGE SWEET POTATO, PEELED AND CUT INTO 1/2-INCH SLICES

1 LARGE DAIKON, PEELED AND CUT INTO 1/2-INCH SLICES

1. To make the braising sauce: Warm the pan over medium heat. Add the soy sauce, red wine, rock sugar, ginger, chiles, garlic, star anise, scallions, orange, and cinnamon sticks. Combine. Add 3 cups of water and bring to a boil. Reduce the heat to low and simmer until the sugar dissolves, 15 to 20 minutes. Taste and add more soy sauce if the flavor lacks depth, or more water if the sauce seems too seasoned.

2. To make the duck and potatoes: Add the duck legs to the braising liquid and simmer until the meat falls from the bones, about 2½ hours. Twenty minutes before the duck is cooked, add the sweet potatoes and daikon. Test the sweet potatoes with a fork to make sure they're tender; if not, simmer a bit longer. Discard the star anise and cinnamon sticks.

3. Serve the duck and vegetables over rice with the braising sauce spooned on top.

Ginger-Orange DUCK "CASSOULET"

FRENCH CASSOULET IS USUALLY MADE with white beans, duck confit, and other ingredients and cooked for hours. This shortcut version uses quick-cooking edamame instead of white beans for a hearty dish that doesn't take all day.

4 DUCK LEGS (LEGS PLUS THIGHS)

KOSHER SALT AND FRESHLY GROUND BLACK PEPPER

1 TABLESPOON GRAPESEED OIL

1 SLICE THICK-CUT BACON

1 MEDIUM ONION, THICKLY SLICED

3 SLICES PEELED GINGER (1/2 INCH THICK), CUT LENGTHWISE FROM A 2- TO 4-INCH PIECE

1 SERRANO PEPPER, HALVED LENGTHWISE

2 MEDIUM UNPEELED ORANGES, WASHED AND QUARTERED

1 CUP BABY CARROTS

2 RIBS CELERY, CUT INTO 1/2-INCH LENGTHS

1 CUP SHELLED EDAMAME

1/4 CUP ORANGE LIQUEUR

2 TABLESPOONS REDUCED-SODIUM SOY SAUCE

1 CUP REDUCED-SODIUM CHICKEN STOCK

1. Preheat the oven to 350°F. Season the duck legs with salt and pepper.

2. Warm the pan over medium-high heat, then add the oil. When the oil is hot, add the duck legs skin-side down. Brown, turning once, for about 20 minutes. If the legs haven't rendered most of their fat, cook a little longer. Transfer the legs to a plate, and pour off the fat.

3. Add the bacon, onions, ginger, and chile. Season with salt and pepper. Sauté until the vegetables have softened slightly, about 2 minutes. Add the oranges, carrots, celery, and edamame, and deglaze the pan with the orange liqueur. Add the soy sauce and stock and adjust the seasonings, if necessary. Return the duck legs to the pan, cover (temperature gauge removed), and bake until a paring knife passes easily through the duck, about 2 hours.

VEAL STEW *with Sweet Peppers*

VEAL MAKES A TENDER, RICH STEW with a mild flavor. If you can't find veal stew meat at your supermarket, you can buy a boneless veal shoulder and ask the butcher to cut it into pieces for you.

1/4 CUP FLOUR

2 POUNDS VEAL STEW MEAT, CUT INTO 1-INCH PIECES

KOSHER SALT AND FRESHLY GROUND BLACK PEPPER

2 TABLESPOONS OLIVE OIL

3 CLOVES GARLIC, FLATTENED

2 TABLESPOONS UNSALTED BUTTER

1 CUP DRY RED WINE

1 TEASPOON DRIED BASIL

1 CAN (14 1/2 OUNCES) WHOLE TOMATOES, WITH JUICE

1 TABLESPOON CRUMBLED DRIED SAGE

2 RED BELL PEPPERS, CUT INTO STRIPS

2 TABLESPOONS DRAINED CAPERS

1. Place the flour in a shallow dish, and dredge the veal in it to coat. Season with salt and pepper.

2. Warm the pan over medium-high heat, then add the oil. Add the garlic and cook for 1 minute. Remove and discard the garlic. Add the butter to the pan and melt. Working in batches, add the veal to the pan and brown, about 3 minutes per side. Using a slotted spoon, transfer the veal to a large bowl.

3. Add the wine, basil, tomatoes with juice, and sage to the pan, breaking up the tomatoes with the back of a spoon and scraping up any browned bits. Return the veal and any accumulated juices to the pan and bring to a boil. Reduce the heat to medium-low, cover, and simmer for 30 minutes.

4. Add the peppers; cover and simmer until the veal and peppers are very tender, stirring frequently, about 50 minutes. Remove from the heat, and stir in the capers. Season with salt and pepper to taste. Serve with crusty bread.

Moroccan LAMB STEW

THIS STEW IS EXOTIC YET COMFORTING, a perfect meal to cook on a lazy Saturday when you have guests coming over. It also keeps well and makes great leftovers—try making sandwiches with the leftover lamb and pita!

2 TABLESPOONS OLIVE OIL

1 LARGE YELLOW ONION, CHOPPED

3 CARROTS, CUBED

6 SMALL POTATOES, PEELED AND CUBED

3 LARGE CLOVES GARLIC, ROUGHLY CHOPPED

2½ POUNDS BONELESS LEG OF LAMB, FAT TRIMMED, CUT INTO CUBES

KOSHER SALT AND FRESHLY GROUND BLACK PEPPER

1 CINNAMON STICK

1 BAY LEAF

1½ TEASPOONS GROUND ALLSPICE

1 TEASPOON RAS EL HANOUT (MOROCCAN SPICE BLEND)

½ TEASPOON GROUND GINGER

6 CANNED ROMA TOMATOES, CUT IN HALF

2½ CUPS REDUCED-SODIUM BEEF BROTH

1. Preheat the oven to 350°F.

2. Warm the pan over medium heat, then add the oil. Add the onions, carrots, and potatoes, and cook for 4 minutes, until the vegetables begin to soften. Add the garlic and cook for 1 minute more. Remove the vegetables from the pan and set aside.

3. Warm the pan (adding more oil if needed), and brown the lamb on all sides. Season with salt and pepper.

4. Increase the heat to medium-high and return the vegetables to the pan. Mix in the cinnamon stick, bay leaf, allspice, ras el hanout, and ginger. Add the tomatoes and broth and bring to a boil for 5 minutes.

5. Cover the pan with the lid (temperature gauge removed), and place the pan in the oven for 1½ to 2 hours. Monitor to add more broth (or water) as needed for the desired consistency. Discard the cinnamon stick and bay leaf. Serve with couscous or pita bread.

ORANGE-GINGER LAMB SHANKS
with Garlic Barley Risotto

THE FLAVORS IN THIS SOUL-WARMING DISH are perfectly balanced and complex—the sweetness and brightness of fresh oranges, the acid and depth of red wine, and the punch from the garlic and chiles will delight your guests and make them wonder what your secret is. You don't need to use a good bottle of wine for this—any less expensive bottle is fine.

2 CUPS PEARL BARLEY

4 LAMB SHANKS, ABOUT 4 POUNDS

KOSHER SALT AND FRESHLY GROUND BLACK PEPPER

2 TABLESPOONS GRAPESEED OIL

2 LARGE ONIONS, ROUGHLY CHOPPED

3 CARROTS, PEELED AND ROUGHLY CHOPPED

3 RIBS CELERY, ROUGHLY CHOPPED

1 BOTTLE DRY RED WINE

5 LARGE UNPEELED ORANGES, 4 WASHED AND QUARTERED, 1 WASHED AND CUT INTO 1/4-INCH SLICES, FOR GARNISH

1/2 CUP REDUCED-SODIUM SOY SAUCE

1 CUP DARK BROWN SUGAR

4 SLICES UNPEELED GINGER (1/4 INCH THICK), CUT LENGTHWISE FROM A 2- TO 4-INCH PIECE

3 DRIED THAI BIRD CHILES

3 CLOVES GARLIC, MINCED

2 TEASPOONS CLARIFIED BUTTER

1. In a large pot, cook the barley in an ample quantity of boiling water until tender, about 45 minutes. Using a large strainer, drain the barley, then run cold tap water through it until it's cold. Drain and set aside.

2. Season the lamb with salt and pepper. Warm the pan over medium-high heat, then add the oil. Add the lamb. Cook on all sides until browned, 8 to 10 minutes. Transfer to a plate.

3. Add the onions, carrots, and celery to the pan, season with salt and pepper, and cook, stirring, until the vegetables have softened, about 3 minutes. Add the wine, deglaze the pot, and simmer until the wine is reduced by a quarter, about 8 minutes. Add the orange quarters, soy sauce, brown sugar, ginger, and chiles. Return the lamb shanks to the pan and add enough water just to cover them. Season with salt and pepper. Bring the liquid to a simmer, cover, and reduce the heat to low. Cook until the meat is falling off the bones, about 3 hours.

4. In a separate pan, sauté the garlic in the butter until tan, add the barley, and season with salt and pepper. Mound the barley on a platter, and top with the lamb. Spoon the braising liquid over the lamb, garnish with the orange slices, and serve.

Foolproof
SPAGHETTI CARBONARA

ENJOY A CLASSIC ROMAN DISH MADE EASY in your stovetop oven! Usually thick sauces like this will stick to the pan and make for a messy cleanup, but not in your Simply Ming pan! The delicious sauce will cling to the pasta, not to the pan.

---

2 EGGS, LIGHTLY BEATEN

3/4 CUP GRATED PARMESAN CHEESE, DIVIDED

1/2 CUP CHOPPED FRESH PARSLEY

1/4 TEASPOON FRESHLY GROUND BLACK PEPPER, PLUS MORE FOR GARNISH

3 TABLESPOONS OLIVE OIL

1/4 POUND PANCETTA, CUT INTO 1/4-INCH SLICES

2 CLOVES GARLIC, CHOPPED

1/2 CUP DRY WHITE WINE

1 POUND SPAGHETTI OR SPAGHETTINI, PREPARED ACCORDING TO PACKAGE DIRECTIONS

1. In a large bowl, combine the eggs, ½ cup of the Parmesan, parsley, and pepper. Set aside.

2. Warm the pan over medium-high heat, then add the oil. Add the pancetta and cook, stirring occasionally, until it starts to brown. Add the garlic and cook, stirring, until fragrant, about 1 minute. Add the wine and cook until the liquid is reduced by half, about 5 minutes. Remove from the heat and set aside.

3. Add the just-prepared pasta to the bowl with the egg mixture. Toss to thoroughly coat. Add the pancetta mixture and toss to combine. Sprinkle with the remaining ¼ cup Parmesan and pepper to taste.

Classic BOLOGNESE SAUCE

THIS HEARTY ITALIAN MEAT SAUCE IS PERFECT for cold winter nights, and just the thing to make your house smell incredible when guests are expected. It's just as good after a month in an airtight container in the freezer as it is right off the stove. Do yourself a favor and make an extra batch and tuck it away for a snowy, busy evening when everyone is hungry.

1/4 CUP OLIVE OIL

2 MEDIUM ONIONS, FINELY CHOPPED

4 RIBS CELERY, FINELY CHOPPED

2 MEDIUM CARROTS, PEELED AND FINELY CHOPPED

5 CLOVES GARLIC, THINLY SLICED

1/4 POUND PANCETTA, THINLY SLICED AND FINELY CHOPPED IN A FOOD PROCESSOR

1 POUND GROUND VEAL

1 POUND 80% LEAN GROUND PORK

1 CAN (6 OUNCES) TOMATO PASTE

1 CUP WHOLE MILK

1 CUP DRY WHITE WINE

1 CUP WATER

1 TEASPOON FRESH THYME

1 1/4 TEASPOONS KOSHER SALT

1/2 TEASPOON FRESHLY GROUND BLACK PEPPER

1. Warm the pan over medium heat, then add the oil. Add the onions, celery, carrots, and garlic. Cook, stirring occasionally, until softened, about 5 minutes.

2. Add the pancetta, veal, and pork. Cook, stirring, until the meat is no longer pink, about 6 minutes.

3. Mix in tomato paste, milk, wine, water, and thyme. Gently simmer, covered, until the sauce is thickened, 1 to 1 1/2 hours. Season with the salt and pepper. Serve over pasta.

Simple PULLED PORK

THIS CROWD-PLEASING RECIPE IS HIGHLIGHTED by a tangy homemade barbecue sauce and an easy spice rub that makes this the best pulled pork you've ever had! You can prepare the rub and the sauce a day ahead, then relax while the pork cooks all afternoon.

SPICE RUB

1 TABLESPOON KOSHER SALT

5 TABLESPOONS DARK BROWN SUGAR

PINCH OF GROUND CAYENNE

1 TEASPOON GROUND CORIANDER

1 TABLESPOON PAPRIKA

1 TEASPOON GROUND CUMIN

1 TEASPOON FRESHLY GROUND BLACK PEPPER

1 WHOLE BONE-IN OR BONELESS PORK BUTT, 5 TO 7 POUNDS

SAUCE

1 CUP TOMATO SAUCE

1/2 CUP DARK MOLASSES

2 TABLESPOONS WORCESTERSHIRE SAUCE

1 TABLESPOON BROWN MUSTARD

2 TEASPOONS HOT SAUCE

1/2 CUP CIDER VINEGAR, DIVIDED

1 TABLESPOON VEGETABLE OIL

1 LARGE ONION, FINELY MINCED

1/2 CUP CHICKEN STOCK

1. Adjust the oven rack to a lower position. Preheat the oven to 300°F.

2. To make the spice rub: In a small bowl, combine the salt, sugar, cayenne, coriander, paprika, cumin, and pepper. Season the pork with 2 to 3 tablespoons of the spice rub, covering it completely. Reserve the remaining spice rub.

3. To make the sauce: In a medium bowl, whisk together the tomato sauce, molasses, Worcestershire sauce, mustard, hot sauce, and 1/4 cup of the cider vinegar.

4. Whisk in the remaining spice rub. Set aside.

5. Warm the pan over medium-high heat, then add the oil. Add the pork and cook, turning occasionally, until well browned on all sides, about 5 minutes. Add the onion, stirring and scraping up any browned bits from the bottom of the pan. Cook until softened, about 2 minutes.

6. Add half of the sauce mixture and the chicken stock. Cover the pan (temperature gauge removed), transfer to the oven, and cook until the pork is just tender, about 4 hours. Remove the lid and continue cooking until a knife or fork shows very little resistance when twisted inside the meat and a dark bark has formed on the outer layer, about 1 hour longer.

7. Transfer the pork to a large bowl, reserving the liquid in the pan. Using a ladle, skim off the excess fat and discard. Add the reserved sauce and remaining ¼ cup vinegar to the pan and whisk to combine. When the pork is cool enough to handle, shred with two forks. Transfer the shredded pork back to the pan and toss with the sauce.

PEPPERED PORK TENDERLOIN *with Sweet and Sour Cranberry—Coconut Sauce*

THIS HEALTHY AND FLAVORFUL PORK RECIPE combines the flavors of fall with Asian flair, making an easy main course that is perfect for the crisp days of autumn. Be careful not to overcook the pork; you want it to still be a little pink in the middle, about 145°F on an instant-read thermometer.

---

2 TABLESPOONS CANOLA OIL, DIVIDED

KOSHER SALT AND FRESHLY GROUND BLACK PEPPER

2 PORK TENDERLOINS, SLICED INTO ½-INCH-THICK MEDALLIONS

1 LARGE ONION, MINCED

½ CUP CHOPPED DRIED CRANBERRIES

1 CUP RICE VINEGAR

1 CUP COCONUT MILK

2 TABLESPOONS FISH SAUCE

1 LARGE SWEET POTATO, COOKED

1. Warm the pan over medium-high heat, and then add 1 tablespoon of the oil. Lightly salt and generously pepper the pork. Add the pork to the pan, and sear on all sides. Reduce the heat to medium and continue cooking until the pork is cooked through; transfer to a platter.

2. In the same pan, add the remaining 1 tablespoon oil, onion, and cranberries, and cook until softened, 2 to 3 minutes. Add the vinegar, and scrape and stir the browned bits from the pan to melt into the liquid. Add the coconut milk and fish sauce and simmer until the sauce is reduced by about a quarter, about 10 minutes. Remove from the heat. Season with salt and pepper to taste.

3. Scoop out some of the sweet potato and surround with the pork. Top with the sauce.

PORK TENDERLOIN
with Maple Glaze

MAPLE SYRUP IS THE PERFECT COMPLEMENT to this tender pork roast flavored with herbs and mustard. The tenderloin is a quick-cooking, forgiving cut of meat (unlike pork loin), but be careful not to overcook it.

2 PORK TENDERLOINS, 12 TO 14 OUNCES EACH

2 TEASPOONS CRUMBLED DRIED SAGE

1 TEASPOON DRIED ROSEMARY

KOSHER SALT AND FRESHLY GROUND BLACK PEPPER

1 TABLESPOON CLARIFIED BUTTER

1/4 CUP LIGHT BROWN SUGAR

2 TEASPOONS DIJON MUSTARD

6 TABLESPOONS APPLE CIDER VINEGAR, DIVIDED

6 TABLESPOONS PURE MAPLE SYRUP, DIVIDED

1. Rub the pork with the sage and rosemary and season with salt and pepper.

2. Warm the pan over medium-high heat, then add the butter. Add the pork and brown on all sides, turning occasionally, about 6 minutes. Reduce the heat to medium-low, cover, and cook, turning occasionally, until a thermometer inserted into the pork registers 150°F, about 10 minutes. Transfer the pork to a platter.

3. In a small bowl, whisk together the sugar, mustard, 4 tablespoons of the vinegar, and 5 tablespoons of the maple syrup. Set aside.

4. Add the remaining 2 tablespoons vinegar to the pan and bring to a boil, scraping up any browned bits. Reduce the heat to medium-low. Return the pork and any accumulated juices to the pan. Add the syrup mixture, turn the pork to coat, and cook for about 2 minutes. Remove from the heat.

5. Transfer the pork to a cutting board or platter. Cut into ½-inch-thick slices. Stir the remaining 1 tablespoon maple syrup into the glaze remaining in the pan. Season the glaze with salt and pepper to taste. Spoon the glaze over the pork slices to serve.

Spice-Rubbed BBQ RIBS

IT'S GAME DAY, AND THE BEST RIBS you've ever had are in your stovetop oven! These easy-to-make ribs come together really quickly, and you can even make the spice rub and BBQ sauce the day before, so you can enjoy your guests (and the game!) while they cook.

SPICE RUB
1/2 CUP DARK BROWN SUGAR

1 TEASPOON ONION POWDER

2 TEASPOONS KOSHER SALT

2 TEASPOONS GROUND CUMIN

2 TEASPOONS CELERY SALT

2 TEASPOONS CHILI POWDER

2 TEASPOON PAPRIKA, SWEET OR SMOKED

1/2 TEASPOON GROUND CAYENNE

1 TEASPOON GARLIC POWDER

3 TO 4 POUNDS PORK BABY BACK RIBS, MEMBRANE REMOVED

BBQ SAUCE
1 CUP KETCHUP

2 TABLESPOONS TOMATO PASTE

3 TABLESPOONS DARK BROWN SUGAR

2 TEASPOONS CHILI POWDER

1/4 TEASPOON GROUND CAYENNE

1/2 TEASPOON ONION POWDER

1/2 TEASPOON GARLIC POWDER

2 TEASPOONS MUSTARD OR 1 TEASPOON DRY MUSTARD POWDER

3 TABLESPOONS RED WINE VINEGAR

1 TEASPOON KOSHER SALT

1 TEASPOON FRESHLY GROUND BLACK PEPPER

1. Preheat the oven to 250°F. Insert the rack for the pan and place it in the oven to heat.

2. To make the spice rub: In a small bowl, mix together the sugar, onion powder, salt, cumin, celery salt, chili powder, paprika, cayenne, and garlic powder. Gently rub the spice mix over the ribs, covering completely. Allow the ribs to sit, refrigerated, in the spice rub for up to 12 hours, or bake them immediately.

3. To make a pouch for the ribs, place two layers of aluminum foil down, and place the ribs (meat-side up) on the foil, then crimp the edges of the foil together around the ribs to wrap them and keep in moisture.

Place the foil pouch on the rack of the pan and cook for 2½ to 3 hours.

4. Turn the oven off and allow the ribs to rest until they're cool enough to handle. Open a corner of the foil pouch and pour the juices into a large measuring cup or a bowl. Set aside. Keep the ribs wrapped in the foil, and return them to the warm oven to free up the pan. Place them directly on a rack.

5. Remove the rack from the pan, and warm the pan over low heat.

6. To make the BBQ sauce: In the pan, add the reserved juices and the ketchup, tomato paste, brown sugar, chili powder, cayenne, onion powder, garlic powder, mustard, vinegar, salt, and pepper. Simmer, stirring frequently, until thickened, about 20 minutes.

7. Remove the ribs from the oven and open the foil pouch. Set the oven to broil. Brush the ribs with the sauce and broil them until the top is caramelized and the sauce is set, 5 to 10 minutes. Allow the ribs to cool slightly before cutting. Serve with extra sauce.

BELL PEPPERS STUFFED
with Spicy Pork Fried Rice

STUFFED PEPPERS ARE A CLASSIC American food, but this version uses a spicy fried rice instead of the usual hamburger mixture, giving them a more sophisticated flavor that is better adapted to modern tastes. They can be put together quickly, though, making them perfect for weeknight suppers.

4 LARGE RED BELL PEPPERS

5 TABLESPOONS CANOLA OIL, PLUS MORE FOR COATING THE PEPPERS

KOSHER SALT AND FRESHLY GROUND BLACK PEPPER

4 LARGE EGGS, BEATEN

1 POUND SPICY ITALIAN SAUSAGE MEAT

1 TABLESPOON MINCED GINGER

1 TABLESPOON MINCED GARLIC

1 JALAPEÑO PEPPER, MINCED

2 BUNCHES SCALLIONS, WHITE AND GREEN PARTS SEPARATED, THINLY SLICED, 3 TABLESPOONS OF GREEN FOR GARNISH

4 CUPS 50/50 WHITE AND BROWN RICE (PAGE 135), COOKED AND COOLED

1 TABLESPOON WHEAT-FREE TAMARI

8 OUNCES FRESH BABY SPINACH

JUICE OF 1 LEMON

1. Preheat the oven to 350°F. Remove the pepper stems and cut off the tops. Mince the tops and set aside. Remove the pepper seeds and ribs. Coat the peppers inside and out with oil, season with salt and pepper, and transfer to the pan. Bake until the peppers have softened, 10 to 12 minutes. Transfer the peppers to a plate; allow the pan to cool to the touch.

2. Cover a large dish with paper towels. Season the eggs with salt and pepper. Warm the pan over high heat, then add 4 tablespoons of the oil. When the oil is almost smoking, add the eggs and scramble, stirring constantly, for about 15 seconds. Transfer the eggs to the paper towels to drain.

3. Warm the pan to medium-high heat, and sauté the sausage meat, breaking it up, until cooked through, 6 to 8 minutes. Transfer to a plate.

4. Rewarm the pan to medium-high heat, then add the remaining 1 tablespoon oil and swirl to coat the pan. When the oil is hot, add the ginger, garlic, jalapeño, and all but the reserved scallion greens. Season with salt and pepper. Add the rice, tamari, eggs, sausage meat, and reserved minced peppers. Heat through, stirring, for 2 to 3 minutes.

5. In a medium bowl, combine the spinach with the lemon juice, season with salt and pepper, and toss. Stuff the peppers with the rice mixture. Place on top of beds of spinach and garnish with the scallion greens.

SHORT RIBS
with Root Vegetables

SHORT RIBS ARE A HEARTY, SATISFYING MEAL that will make your whole house smell great while they cook! Perfect for a cold winter day, these ribs have some spice from the chili powder and depth of flavor from the soy sauce. Make sure to keep the liquid at a simmer, not a full boil, while the ribs cook.

1½ CUPS FLOUR

1 TABLESPOON CHILI POWDER

6 SHORT RIBS

KOSHER SALT AND FRESHLY GROUND BLACK PEPPER

3 TABLESPOONS GRAPESEED OIL, DIVIDED

2 ONIONS, CHOPPED

2 TABLESPOONS MINCED GARLIC

1 POUND BABY CARROTS

6 RIBS CELERY, SPLIT LENGTHWISE AND HALVED IF LARGE

1 CELERIAC (CELERY ROOT), PEELED AND CUT INTO 1-INCH DICE

1 LARGE SWEET POTATO, PEELED AND CUT INTO 1-INCH PIECES

1 LARGE PARSNIP, PEELED AND CUT INTO 1-INCH PIECES

2 TABLESPOONS REDUCED-SODIUM SOY SAUCE

1. In a large shallow dish, combine the flour and chili powder. Season the ribs with salt and pepper and dredge in the flour mixture.

2. Warm the pan over medium heat, then add 2 tablespoons of the oil. When the oil is hot, shake the excess flour mixture from the ribs, add them to the pan, and cook, turning once, until browned, about 8 minutes. Set the ribs aside.

3. Add the remaining 1 tablespoon oil to the pan, and swirl to coat the bottom. Add the onions and garlic and sauté, stirring, for about 3 minutes. Add the carrots, celery, celeriac, sweet potato, and parsnip. Season with salt and pepper. Add the ribs, soy sauce, and enough water to almost cover the ingredients. Taste and adjust the seasoning, if necessary. Cover and cook over low heat until a paring knife passes through the meat easily, about 1½ hours.

Just-Like-Mom's
RICOTTA MEATBALLS

EVERY HOME COOK SHOULD HAVE a back-pocket meatball recipe—here's yours. It's easy, foolproof, and a cinch to make in your stovetop oven. Rock it old-school and serve over spaghetti, or tuck the meatballs into a hot loaf of garlic bread right out of the oven to make the sandwich of your dreams.

2 TABLESPOONS OLIVE OIL

1 POUND 80% LEAN GROUND BEEF

1 POUND GROUND VEAL

1 CUP RICOTTA CHEESE

2 LARGE EGGS

1/2 CUP BREAD CRUMBS

1/4 CUP CHOPPED FRESH PARSLEY

1 TABLESPOON CHOPPED FRESH OREGANO OR 1 TEASPOON DRIED OREGANO

2 TEASPOONS KOSHER SALT

1/4 TEASPOON RED PEPPER FLAKES

1/2 TEASPOON DRIED BASIL

4 CUPS TOMATO SAUCE

1. Preheat the oven to 450°F. Drizzle the olive oil into the pan, and brush to evenly coat. Set aside.

2. In a large bowl, mix the beef, veal, ricotta, eggs, bread crumbs, parsley, oregano, salt, red pepper flakes, and basil until thoroughly combined. Roll 2 tablespoons of the mixture into a ball and place it in the pan. Repeat with the remaining mixture.

3. Bake for 20 minutes, or until the meatballs are cooked through and a thermometer inserted into the center of a meatball registers 165°F. Remove the pan from the oven and carefully drain off any grease. Pour the tomato sauce over the meatballs. Return the pan to the oven for 15 minutes.

Chunky BEEF RAGU

MEAT SAUCE IS NOT ONLY A DELICIOUS STAR of the show on linguine or rigatoni, but it's also a versatile ingredient to have on hand. Add to a risotto or mac 'n' cheese for a meaty kick, or even toss with your kids' vegetables to make them beg for more.

1/4 CUP OLIVE OIL

3 POUNDS BEEF CHUCK STEAK, CUT INTO 2-INCH CHUNKS

KOSHER SALT AND FRESHLY GROUND BLACK PEPPER

4 SHALLOTS, CHOPPED

3 CLOVES GARLIC, CRUSHED

2 CARROTS, PEELED AND THICKLY SLICED

2 RIBS CELERY, THICKLY SLICED

3 FRESH THYME SPRIGS

2 FRESH ROSEMARY SPRIGS

2 BAY LEAVES

1 CUP DRY RED WINE

2 TABLESPOONS TOMATO PASTE

1 CAN (28 OUNCES) DICED TOMATOES

1 CUP BEEF STOCK

1 1/2 CUPS COLD WATER

1. Warm the pan over medium heat, then add the oil. Season the beef with salt and pepper. Add the beef in batches to the pan and cook for 4 to 5 minutes or until browned all over. Transfer to a bowl.

2. Add the shallots, garlic, carrots, and celery to the pan. Cook for 3 minutes or until starting to brown. Add the thyme, rosemary, and bay leaves. Cook for 1 to 2 minutes or until fragrant. Add the wine. Cook for 2 minutes or until reduced by half.

3. Return the beef to the pan. Add the tomato paste, tomatoes, stock, and water. Bring to a boil, then reduce the heat to low. Cook, covered, for 2 hours or until the beef is tender. Discard the thyme sprigs, rosemary sprigs, and bay leaves.

Game-Day
BEEF AND BEER CHILI

THIS HOMESTYLE CHILI comes together in less than an hour, so you can even make it on a weeknight. The leftovers make fantastic nachos or taco filling.

5 POUNDS
GROUND CHUCK

2 TABLESPOONS
CANOLA OIL

6 LARGE ONIONS,
COARSELY CHOPPED

4 LARGE RED BELL
PEPPERS, SEEDED, CUT
INTO 1/2-INCH PIECES

4 LARGE YELLOW BELL
PEPPERS, SEEDED, CUT
INTO 1/2-INCH PIECES

2 LARGE JALAPEÑO
PEPPERS WITH SEEDS,
CHOPPED

1 1/2 TABLESPOONS
GROUND CUMIN

1 TABLESPOON
GROUND CORIANDER

7 TABLESPOONS
CHILI POWDER

2 TABLESPOONS PAPRIKA

2 CANS (28 OUNCES)
CRUSHED TOMATOES

2 CANS (15 OUNCES)
KIDNEY BEANS, DRAINED
AND RINSED

1 BOTTLE (12 OUNCES),
DARK BEER, SUCH AS
STOUT

KOSHER SALT AND
FRESHLY GROUND
BLACK PEPPER

SOUR CREAM,
FOR TOPPING

CHOPPED SCALLIONS,
FOR TOPPING

SHREDDED CHEDDAR
CHEESE, FOR TOPPING

1. Warm the pan over medium-high heat, then add the beef. Cook until the beef is cooked through, about 8 minutes. Remove the beef to a large bowl; wipe out the cooled pan.

2. Rewarm the pan over medium-high heat, then add the oil. Add the onions, peppers, and jalapeños. Cook until the vegetables soften, about 15 minutes.

Add the beef back to the pan. Mix in the cumin, coriander, chili powder, and paprika. Add the tomatoes, beans, and beer and bring to a boil. Reduce the heat and simmer for 20 minutes, stirring often. Season with salt and pepper to taste.

3. Top with sour cream, scallions, and Cheddar.

CLASSIC BEEF STEW
with Red Wine

THE STOVETOP OVEN IS PERFECT FOR STEWS, because the sloped sides and domed lid capture all of the flavors and moisture, so your stew is silky, rich, and delicious.

3 TABLESPOONS
VEGETABLE OIL

3 POUNDS BONELESS
CHUCK ROAST, CUT
INTO 2-INCH PIECES

2 TEASPOONS
KOSHER SALT

1 TABLESPOON FRESHLY
GROUND BLACK PEPPER

2 YELLOW ONIONS, CUT
INTO 1-INCH CHUNKS

1/4 CUP FLOUR

4 CLOVES GARLIC,
MINCED

2 CUPS RED WINE

3 CUPS BEEF BROTH

1/2 TEASPOON
DRIED ROSEMARY

1 BAY LEAF

1/2 TEASPOON
DRIED THYME

6 YUKON GOLD POTATOES,
CUT INTO 1-INCH CUBES

4 CARROTS, PEELED AND
CUT INTO 1-INCH SLICES

2 RIBS CELERY, CUT
INTO 1/2-INCH SLICES

FRESH PARSLEY,
FOR GARNISH

1. Warm the pan over medium-high heat, then add the oil. Add the beef, season with the salt and pepper, and brown on all sides. Remove with a slotted spoon and set aside.

2. Add the onions and cook until softened, about 5 minutes. Reduce the heat to medium-low, and add the flour. Cook for 2 minutes, stirring often. Add the garlic and cook for 1 minute, until fragrant. Add the wine and deglaze the pan, scraping any brown bits stuck to the bottom of the pan. Simmer for 5 minutes, then add the broth, rosemary, bay leaf, thyme, and beef. Bring back to a simmer, cover, and cook for about 1 hour.

3. Add the potatoes, carrots, and celery. Simmer, covered, for 30 minutes or until the meat and vegetables are tender. Remove from heat and let rest for 15 minutes before serving. Discard the bay leaf. Garnish with parsley.

Stovetop ROPA VIEJA

TRY THIS DELICIOUS SOUTH-OF-THE-BORDER recipe for a succulent braised meat that can be folded into tortillas or served over rice. It will warm up your evening—and free it up too, because it practically cooks itself through simmering.

2 TABLESPOONS OLIVE OIL

3 POUNDS SKIRT OR FLANK STEAK, TRIMMED

KOSHER SALT AND FRESHLY GROUND BLACK PEPPER

1 YELLOW ONION, THINLY SLICED

1 RED BELL PEPPER, THINLY SLICED

1 YELLOW BELL PEPPER, THINLY SLICED

4 CLOVES GARLIC, CHOPPED

1 TABLESPOON GROUND CUMIN

1 TABLESPOON DRIED THYME

1 TABLESPOON DRIED OREGANO

1 CUP BEEF STOCK

1 CAN (14 OUNCES) DICED TOMATOES, WITH JUICE

1 CAN (6 OUNCES) TOMATO SAUCE

2 BAY LEAVES

1. Warm the pan over medium-high heat, then add the oil. Season the steak with salt and pepper, then add to the pan and brown, about 2 minutes per side. Remove the steak from the pan (keep the drippings in). Set aside.

2. In the pan, add the onion and peppers. Reduce the heat to medium and cook for 15 to 20 minutes until the onions are caramelized. Add the garlic, cumin, thyme, and oregano, and cook for 1 minute. Add the broth and bring it to a rapid boil, scraping up the browned bits on the bottom of the pan. Add the diced tomatoes, tomato sauce, and bay leaves. Simmer for 5 minutes.

3. Return the steak to the pan. Bring to a boil, then reduce the heat to low. Cover and simmer 2 to 3 hours or until the beef is fork tender and falls apart easily. Discard the bay leaves. Transfer the steak to a plate and shred it. Season with salt and pepper to taste.

Grown-Up SLOPPY JOES

THIS EASY RECIPE IS SO MUCH BETTER than the stuff in the can! A crowd-pleaser that is delicious piled high on toasted buns, this meaty mixture is great for game-day parties or weekday suppers. Adults love this as much as kids do, and it's a great dish to bring to a potluck dinner—just grab rolls and let people make their own sandwiches.

2 TABLESPOONS
CLARIFIED BUTTER

1 LARGE ONION, CHOPPED

4 CLOVES GARLIC,
FINELY CHOPPED

1 MEDIUM CARROT,
PEELED AND FINELY
CHOPPED

1 RIB CELERY,
FINELY CHOPPED

1 TEASPOON
KOSHER SALT, DIVIDED

1½ POUNDS
GROUND CHUCK

1 TABLESPOON
CHILI POWDER

1 TEASPOON
GROUND CUMIN

¾ TEASPOON FRESHLY
GROUND BLACK PEPPER

½ CUP DRY RED WINE

2 TABLESPOONS
WORCESTERSHIRE SAUCE

¼ CUP KETCHUP

1½ TABLESPOONS
PACKED BROWN SUGAR

4 KAISER ROLLS, SPLIT

1. Warm the pan over medium-high heat, then add the butter. Add the onion and garlic. Cook, stirring occasionally, until the onion begins to soften, 4 to 5 minutes. Add the carrot, celery, and ½ teaspoon of the salt. Cook, stirring occasionally, until the vegetables soften, 4 to 5 minutes.

2. Add the beef and brown, breaking up lumps, for 5 to 6 minutes. Add the chili powder, cumin, remaining ½ teaspoon salt, and pepper and cook, stirring, for 2 minutes. Add the wine, Worcestershire sauce, ketchup, and brown sugar. Bring to a boil, stirring occasionally, until the sauce has thickened, about 6 minutes. Serve on rolls.

Andouille Sausage and
SHRIMP JAMBALAYA

JAMBALAYA IS A FANTASTIC ONE-DISH MEAL that is perfect for potlucks or any party where the food needs to be served at room temperature, because this delicious concoction is just as good that way as it is hot off the stove. The rice, shrimp, and sausage create a perfect complement of flavors, and won't stick to the special finish on your Simply Ming Stovetop Oven!

1 TABLESPOON OLIVE OIL

1 CUP CHOPPED ONION

1 CUP CHOPPED
RED BELL PEPPER

1 TABLESPOON
MINCED GARLIC

6 OUNCES ANDOUILLE
SAUSAGE, SLICED

1 CUP UNCOOKED
LONG-GRAIN WHITE RICE

1 TEASPOON PAPRIKA

1 TEASPOON FRESHLY
GROUND BLACK PEPPER

1 TEASPOON
DRIED OREGANO

1/2 TEASPOON
DRIED THYME

1/2 TEASPOON
ONION POWDER

1/4 TEASPOON
GARLIC SALT

1 BAY LEAF

2 CUPS CHICKEN BROTH

3/4 CUP WATER

1 TABLESPOON
TOMATO PASTE

1/2 TEASPOON
HOT PEPPER SAUCE

1 CAN (14.5 OUNCES)
NO-SALT-ADDED DICED
TOMATOES, WITH JUICE

1/2 POUND MEDIUM
SHRIMP, PEELED
AND DEVEINED

2 TABLESPOONS
CHOPPED FRESH PARSLEY

1. Warm the pan over medium heat, then add the oil. Add the onion, pepper, garlic, and sausage, and cook for 5 minutes, or until the vegetables are tender.

2. Add the rice, paprika, pepper, oregano, thyme, onion powder, garlic salt, and bay leaf. Cook for 2 minutes.

3. Add the broth, water, tomato paste, hot pepper sauce, and diced tomatoes, and bring to a boil. Cover, reduce the heat to low, and simmer for 20 minutes.

4. Add the shrimp and cook for 5 minutes. Remove from the heat and let stand for 5 minutes. Discard the bay leaf. Stir in the parsley.

SHRIMP SCAMPI
Over Spaghetti

THIS SUPER-FAST WEEKNIGHT MEAL serves up antioxidants and healthy fats while indulging your family with a delicious Italian classic. Peel the shrimp in the morning and stash in a bowl in the fridge to make prep even easier.

4 CLOVES GARLIC, 2 GRATED AND 2 THINLY SLICED

1 TEASPOON KOSHER SALT

3 TABLESPOONS OLIVE OIL, DIVIDED

1 POUND LARGE SHRIMP, PEELED AND DEVEINED

1/4 TEASPOON RED PEPPER FLAKES

1 CUP CHERRY TOMATOES, HALVED

1/4 CUP DRY WHITE WINE

1 TABLESPOON FRESH LEMON JUICE

1/4 CUP (1/2 STICK) UNSALTED BUTTER

1 POUND SPAGHETTI, PREPARED PER PACKAGE DIRECTIONS

1/4 CUP GRATED PARMESAN CHEESE

3 TABLESPOONS CHOPPED FRESH BASIL

1. In a medium bowl, combine the grated garlic, salt, and 1 tablespoon of the oil. Add the shrimp and toss to coat. Chill, uncovered, for at least 30 minutes and up to 1 hour.

2. Warm the pan over medium heat, then add the remaining 2 tablespoons oil. Add the shrimp mixture and cook until the shrimp are just pink, about 1 minute per side. Transfer the shrimp to a plate with a slotted spoon, leaving as much oil in the pan as possible.

3. Add the sliced garlic and red pepper flakes to the pan and cook until fragrant, about 1 minute. Add the tomatoes, wine, and lemon juice and cook, stirring occasionally, until reduced by half, about 2 minutes. Add the butter and cook, stirring occasionally, until the butter is melted and the sauce is thickened, about 5 minutes.

4. Transfer the shrimp and any juices back to the pan. Stir and cook until the shrimp are fully warmed through, about 2 minutes. Serve over spaghetti. Top with Parmesan and basil.

Creamy Garlic SHRIMP RISOTTO

THIS DELICIOUS RISOTTO IS A CINCH to make in the stovetop oven, because the starchy rice won't stick to the pan! You can use other seafood in addition to the shrimp—feel free to stir some cooked bay scallops, crabmeat, or lobster chunks into the risotto at the end of cooking.

---

6 CUPS REDUCED-SODIUM CHICKEN BROTH

1 CUP DRY WHITE WINE, DIVIDED

6 TABLESPOONS CLARIFIED BUTTER, DIVIDED

1 POUND UNCOOKED LARGE SHRIMP, PEELED AND DEVEINED

1/4 TEASPOON RED PEPPER FLAKES

2 TEASPOONS MINCED GARLIC, DIVIDED

3/4 CUP FINELY CHOPPED ONION

2 CUPS ARBORIO RICE

2 TABLESPOONS PLUS 2 TEASPOONS CHOPPED FRESH PARSLEY, DIVIDED

KOSHER SALT AND FRESHLY GROUND BLACK PEPPER

1. In a medium saucepan, heat the chicken broth and 1/4 cup of the wine until simmering, and keep hot.

2. Warm the pan over medium heat, then melt 2 tablespoons of the butter. Add the shrimp, red pepper flakes, and 1 teaspoon of the garlic. Sauté until the shrimp begin to turn pink, about 2 minutes. Add the remaining 3/4 cup wine. Simmer until the shrimp are just cooked through, about 2 minutes. Drain the shrimp and set aside; reserve the cooking liquid.

3. In the pan over medium heat, melt the remaining 4 tablespoons butter. Add the onion and remaining 1 teaspoon garlic; sauté until the onion is golden, about 4 minutes.

Add the rice and stir to coat, about 2 minutes. Slowly add the broth-wine mixture, a little at a time, simmering until the liquid is absorbed before adding more. Stir often and add more only when all the liquid is absorbed. This will take about 20 minutes. Stir in the reserved shrimp cooking liquid.

Cook until the rice is just tender and the mixture is creamy, about 5 minutes. Remove from the heat.

4. Mix the shrimp and 2 tablespoons of the parsley into the risotto. Season with salt and pepper to taste. Garnish with the remaining 2 teaspoons parsley.

Teriyaki SHRIMP STIR-FRY

HERE'S AN EASY STIR-FRY with a simple homemade teriyaki sauce that tastes so much better than bottled! Your family will think you toiled all day, but this recipe comes together in just a few minutes. Add some rice and a salad, and you have an easy meal that tastes better and costs less than takeout.

TERIYAKI SAUCE

1/4 CUP REDUCED-SODIUM SOY SAUCE

1/2 CUP WATER

3 TABLESPOONS DARK BROWN SUGAR

2 TEASPOONS MINCED GARLIC

2 TEASPOONS MINCED GINGER

1 TABLESPOON HONEY

1 TEASPOON TOASTED SESAME OIL

1 TABLESPOON PLUS 1 TEASPOON CORNSTARCH

STIR-FRY

3 TEASPOONS VEGETABLE OIL, DIVIDED

1 RED BELL PEPPER, CHOPPED

KOSHER SALT AND FRESHLY GROUND BLACK PEPPER

1/2 CUP CHOPPED SCALLION

1 1/4 POUNDS LARGE SHRIMP, PEELED AND DEVEINED

SESAME SEEDS, FOR GARNISH

SLICED SCALLIONS, FOR GARNISH

1. To make the sauce: Warm the pan over medium-high heat, then add the soy sauce, water, brown sugar, garlic, ginger, honey, and sesame oil. Stir until the brown sugar is dissolved, about 3 minutes. Increase the heat to high and bring to a boil.

2. Mix the cornstarch with 2 tablespoons of cold water until dissolved. Add the cornstarch mixture to the sauce and boil for 1 to 2 minutes or until the sauce has thickened. Transfer to a bowl and set aside.

3. To make the stir-fry: Wipe out the pan. Warm the pan over medium-high heat, then add 1 teaspoon of the vegetable oil. Add the bell pepper. Season with salt and pepper. Cook for 2 to 3 minutes until the pepper starts to soften. Add the scallions and cook for 1 minute. Remove the vegetables from the pan and set aside.

4. Wipe out the pan. Warm the pan over high heat, then add the remaining 2 teaspoons oil.

5. Place the shrimp in the pan and season with salt and pepper. Cook for 2 to 3 minutes or until the shrimp are pink.

6. Transfer the vegetables back to the pan. Pour the sauce over the top and cook for 1 to 2 minutes over medium-high heat until warmed through. Serve over rice, and garnish with sesame seeds and sliced scallions.

Thai SHRIMP SOUP

FOR THOSE NIGHTS WHEN YOU'RE CRAVING a bowl of soup but don't have all day to cook, fire up your stovetop oven and make this delicious Thai soup with shrimp, coconut, and ginger! The strong flavors perfectly complement the mild shrimp, and nobody will believe how quickly you made such a delicious soup.

---

2 TABLESPOONS CLARIFIED BUTTER

1 POUND MEDIUM SHRIMP, PEELED AND DEVEINED

KOSHER SALT AND FRESHLY GROUND BLACK PEPPER

2 CLOVES GARLIC, MINCED

1 ONION, DICED

1 RED BELL PEPPER, JULIENNED

1 TABLESPOON GRATED FRESH GINGER

2 TABLESPOONS RED CURRY PASTE

2 CANS (12 OUNCES) UNSWEETENED COCONUT MILK

4 CUPS VEGETABLE STOCK

JUICE OF 1 LIME

1/2 CUP CHOPPED THAI BASIL, FOR GARNISH

---

1. Warm the pan over medium-high heat, then melt the butter. Add the shrimp and season with salt and pepper. Cook, stirring occasionally, until the shrimp turn pink, 2 to 3 minutes. Transfer to a plate and set aside.

2. Add the garlic, onion, and pepper to the pan. Cook, stirring occasionally, until softened, 3 to 4 minutes. Stir in the ginger and cook until fragrant, about 1 minute.

3. Whisk in the curry paste until well combined, and cook for about 1 minute. Gradually whisk in the coconut milk and vegetable stock, and cook, whisking constantly until incorporated, 1 to 2 minutes. Bring to a boil; reduce the heat and simmer until slightly thickened, 8 to 10 minutes. Add the shrimp back to the soup. Drizzle with the lime juice and garnish with the Thai basil.

Savory Shrimp LOBSTER BOIL

BRING THE BEACH HOME with this delicious—and easy to make—seafood dish! With just a few ingredients, you can create an impressive one-dish meal that is good for you, too. If you use larger lobsters, you may need to adjust the cooking time to ensure they're done, and frozen lobster tails work, too—just simmer them until they're opaque before adding the shrimp.

2 TEASPOONS GRAPESEED OIL

1 YELLOW ONION, SLICED

4 RIBS CELERY, CUT INTO 1-INCH SLICES

KOSHER SALT AND FRESHLY GROUND BLACK PEPPER

2 LEMONS, HALVED

1 BAY LEAF

5 FRESH THYME SPRIGS

1 CUP DRY WHITE WINE

6 NEW POTATOES, CUT IN HALF

2 EARS CORN, CUT INTO THIRDS

2 LOBSTERS, EACH 1¼ POUNDS

1 POUND SHRIMP

1. Warm the pan over medium heat, then add the oil. Add the onion and celery and cook for 3 to 4 minutes until softened. Season with kosher salt and freshly ground black pepper to taste. Add the lemons, bay leaf, thyme, wine, and enough water to cover. Bring to a boil.

2. Add the potatoes, reduce the heat to low, and simmer for 10 minutes. Add the corn, and simmer for 5 minutes. Add the lobster and simmer for 15 minutes. Add the shrimp and simmer just until pink. Discard the lemons, bay leaf, and thyme sprigs. Remove the lobsters from the liquid and divide the liquid, vegetables, and shrimp between 2 bowls to serve.

Tea-Smoked SALMON

DID YOU KNOW YOU CAN USE YOUR STOVETOP OVEN as a mini-smoker? Making your own smoked salmon is easier than you think. With just a few ingredients and 30 minutes, you can make impressive homemade smoked salmon that is far better than any you can buy.

---

1 POUND SKINLESS SALMON FILLET, CUT INTO 4 EQUAL PIECES

1 CUP PLUS 1 TABLESPOON SUGAR, DIVIDED

1/2 CUP MIRIN

1/2 CUP WATER

1 PIECE (4 INCHES) FRESH GINGER, JULIENNED

1 TABLESPOON KOSHER SALT

1 TEASPOON TOASTED SZECHUAN PEPPERCORNS

1 CUP LONG-GRAIN RICE

1 CUP OOLONG TEA

1. Place the salmon in a baking dish. In a medium bowl, combine the 1 tablespoon sugar, mirin, water, ginger, salt, and peppercorns. Stir until the salt and sugar dissolve. Pour the mixture over the salmon, cover, and allow to brine, refrigerated, for about 1 hour.

2. Line the pan with foil, fitting it closely against the pan's interior. Add the rice, remaining 1 cup sugar, and tea. Heat the pan over medium heat until the rice mixture begins to smoke.

3. Remove the salmon from the brining mixture and place it on the pan rack. Dampen 2 dishcloths. Fit the rack into the pan, and put the lid on. Fold and wrap the towels around the juncture of the pan and the lid to make a seal. Turn the heat to low, and smoke the salmon for 15 minutes. Turn off the heat and smoke the salmon for 15 minutes more. The salmon will be cooked medium-rare to medium.

One-Pan
TERIYAKI SALMON

ONE PAN MEANS FEWER DISHES and less mess, and this easy marinated salmon takes just minutes to prepare. The sweet and pungent glaze makes this salmon almost addictive—just serve with rice to enjoy every last bit of the sauce!

1 CLOVE GARLIC, MINCED

1/2 TEASPOON MINCED FRESH GINGER

2 TABLESPOONS REDUCED-SODIUM SOY SAUCE

1/4 CUP REDUCED-SODIUM TERIYAKI SAUCE

2 TABLESPOONS WATER

2 TABLESPOONS DARK BROWN SUGAR

1 TABLESPOON RICE WINE VINEGAR

1 TEASPOON SESAME OIL

4 SKINLESS SALMON FILLETS

1 TABLESPOON VEGETABLE OIL

1 TEASPOON CORNSTARCH

SCALLIONS, FOR GARNISH

SESAME SEEDS, FOR GARNISH

1. In a medium bowl, combine the garlic, ginger, soy sauce, teriyaki sauce, water, brown sugar, vinegar, and sesame oil. Reserve half of the marinade and add the rest to a ziplock bag. Place the salmon in the bag and marinate, refrigerated, for 1 hour.

2. Warm the pan over medium heat, then add the vegetable oil. Add the salmon, discarding the marinade in the bag, and cook for 3 to 4 minutes per side. Remove the salmon from the pan and set aside, keeping warm.

3. Add the reserved marinade to the pan and bring to a simmer.

4. In a small bowl, whisk together the cornstarch and 1 tablespoon cold water. Slowly whisk in the cornstarch mixture to the marinade and simmer until thickened. Serve the salmon drizzled with the teriyaki sauce. Garnish with the scallions and sesame seeds.

OLIVE OIL-POACHED SALMON *with Tomato Tapenade*

THIS SILKY SALMON DISH HAS A BRIGHT PUNCH of flavor—and a kick of healthy superfoods—from the olive tapenade. Cooking salmon this way ensures it won't dry out.

1 CUP OLIVE OIL

1 TABLESPOON FERMENTED BLACK BEANS

1 CUP PITTED NIÇOISE OLIVES OR OIL-CURED BLACK OLIVES

1 LARGE ONION, THINLY SLICED

1 CAN (28 OUNCES) ROMA TOMATOES, DRAINED, CRUSHED BY HAND TO REMOVE AS MUCH JUICE AS POSSIBLE, AND COARSELY CHOPPED

KOSHER SALT AND FRESHLY GROUND BLACK PEPPER

4 SKINLESS SALMON FILLETS (6 TO 8 OUNCES), CUT INTO 5-INCH STRIPS

1/4 CUP CHOPPED THAI BASIL OR REGULAR BASIL

3 CUPS FRESH BABY ARUGULA

3 LEMONS, JUICE OF 1, ZEST OF ANOTHER, THE THIRD CUT INTO WEDGES

1. Preheat the oven to 300°F.

2. Warm the pan to medium heat, then add the oil. Add the black beans, olives, and onion, and simmer until the onion begins to soften, about 3 minutes. Add the tomatoes, season with salt and pepper, and cook for 8 minutes. Transfer three-fourths of the tapenade mixture to a medium bowl.

3. Season the salmon with salt and pepper. Add the salmon to the pan and top with the basil. Spoon the remaining tapenade over the fish until it is submerged. Cover with the lid (temperature gauge removed) and bake the salmon for 8 to 10 minutes.

4. Place a handful of the arugula on individual plates, drizzle with the lemon juice, and season with salt and pepper. Using a slotted spoon, place the salmon on the arugula. Top with the tapenade. Garnish with the lemon zest. and place a lemon wedge alongside.

SALMON PASTA
with Cherry Tomato Sauce

EVERYONE LOVES SALMON, and this is a great new way to prepare it. The spicy sauce and crunchy pine nuts add fantastic flavor and texture.

3 TABLESPOONS OLIVE OIL, DIVIDED

4 OIL-PACKED ANCHOVY FILLETS

4 CLOVES GARLIC, SLICED

1/2 TEASPOON RED PEPPER FLAKES

2 PINTS CHERRY TOMATOES, HALVED, DIVIDED

KOSHER SALT AND FRESHLY GROUND BLACK PEPPER

1 POUND SKINLESS SALMON FILLET

1/4 CUP PINE NUTS

1 POUND PENNE PASTA

1/2 CUP CHOPPED FRESH PARSLEY, DIVIDED

1. Warm the pan over medium heat, then add 2 tablespoons of the oil. Add the anchovies, garlic, and red pepper flakes and cook, stirring, until the anchovies disintegrate, about 3 minutes. Add half of the tomatoes. Season with salt and pepper. Cook, stirring occasionally, until the sauce thickens, 12 to 15 minutes. Add the remaining tomatoes. Remove from the heat and transfer to a bowl.

2. Warm the remaining 1 tablespoon oil in the pan over medium-high heat. Season the salmon with salt and pepper and cook until browned and just cooked through, about 4 minutes per side. Remove to a plate to cool slightly, then flake the flesh.

3. Wipe out the cooled pan, then warm it over medium-low heat. Add the pine nuts to toast, tossing often until golden brown, about 4 minutes. Remove to a plate to cool.

4. In a large pot of boiling salted water, cook the pasta, stirring occasionally, until al dente. Drain, reserving 1 cup cooking liquid. In the pan, combine the pasta, 1/2 cup of the pasta cooking liquid, and the tomato sauce. Cook over low heat, tossing often and adding cooking liquid as needed, until the sauce is thickened and coats the pasta. Add the salmon and pine nuts along with half of the parsley and toss to combine. Garnish with the remaining parsley.

SPAGHETTI *alle Vongole*

A RESTAURANT FAVORITE, THIS EASY PASTA recipe is super simple to make at home. If you can't find fresh clams, you can substitute two cans of baby clams, with their juice—just add them to the pan and leave them in there rather than removing them to a bowl.

KOSHER SALT

1 POUND SPAGHETTI

4 TABLESPOONS OLIVE OIL

2 CLOVES GARLIC, CHOPPED

1/4 TEASPOON RED PEPPER FLAKES

1/2 CUP WHITE WINE

3 POUNDS CHERRYSTONE OR LITTLENECK CLAMS, SCRUBBED

1/4 CUP GRATED PARMESAN CHEESE

2 TABLESPOONS CHOPPED FRESH PARSLEY

1. In a large pot, bring 3 quarts of salted water to a boil. Cook the spaghetti, stirring occasionally, until barely tender. Drain, reserving ½ cup of the pasta cooking water.

2. Warm the pan over medium heat, then add the oil. Add the garlic and cook for about 1 minute, until golden. Add the red pepper flakes and cook for 15 seconds. Add the wine and clams, and increase the heat to high. Cover and cook until the clams open and release their juices, 3 to 6 minutes. As clams open, use tongs to transfer them to a bowl. Discard any clams that don't open.

3. Add ¼ cup of the reserved pasta water to the pan. Bring to a boil. Add the spaghetti to the pan. Cook over high heat, tossing constantly, until the pasta is al dente. Add the Parmesan, clams (plus any juices), parsley, and any additional pasta water needed. Toss to combine.

New England CLAM CHOWDER

THERE IS A FIERCE BATTLE BETWEEN those who prefer tomato-based Manhattan clam chowder and those who prefer the classic cream-based version. This flavorful bowl of comfort is guaranteed to bring you to the creamy side. And it can be yours in one pan for a delicious lunch or dinner.

---

4 BACON STRIPS

2 RIBS CELERY, CHOPPED

1 LARGE ONION, CHOPPED

1 CLOVE GARLIC, MINCED

3 SMALL POTATOES, PEELED AND CUBED

1 CUP WATER

1 BOTTLE (8 OUNCES) CLAM JUICE

1 TABLESPOON REDUCED-SODIUM CHICKEN BOUILLON GRANULES

1/4 TEASPOON WHITE PEPPER

1/4 TEASPOON DRIED THYME

1/3 CUP FLOUR

2 CUPS FAT-FREE HALF-AND-HALF, DIVIDED

2 CANS (6 1/2 OUNCES) CHOPPED CLAMS, UNDRAINED

1. Warm the pan over medium heat. Add the bacon and cook until crisp. Remove to a plate lined with a paper towel to drain.

2. Add the celery and onion to the bacon drippings in the pan, and cook until softened, 2 to 3 minutes. Add the garlic, and cook for 1 minute longer. Stir in the potatoes, water, clam juice, bouillon, pepper, and thyme. Bring to a boil. Reduce the heat to low. Simmer for 15 to 20 minutes or until the potatoes are tender.

3. In a small bowl, mix the flour and 1 cup of the half-and-half until smooth. Gradually stir the mixture into the soup. Bring to a boil; cook and stir for 1 to 2 minutes or until thickened.

4. Stir in the clams and remaining 1 cup half-and-half; heat through (do not boil). Crumble the bacon, and sprinkle atop each serving.

BEER-STEAMED
Mussels with Chorizo

CHORIZO IS A SPICY SPANISH SAUSAGE that is available in most supermarkets, but feel free to swap it with Andouille or other spicy sausage. Be sure to serve this with some crusty bread to mop up all of the delicious broth.

1 TABLESPOON OLIVE OIL

8 OUNCES CHORIZO, CASINGS REMOVED

1 MEDIUM WHITE ONION, THINLY SLICED

2 CLOVES GARLIC, FINELY CHOPPED

1¼ TEASPOONS GROUND CUMIN

1 TEASPOON KOSHER SALT

1 BOTTLE (12 OUNCES) BEER

2 TABLESPOONS UNSALTED BUTTER

2 POUNDS MUSSELS, SCRUBBED AND DEBEARDED

½ CUP COARSELY CHOPPED CILANTRO

1. Warm the pan over medium heat, then add the oil. Add the chorizo, onion, garlic, cumin, and salt. Cook, stirring frequently, breaking up the chorizo, until the onions are softened and the chorizo is cooked through, about 10 minutes.

2. Add the beer and butter. Increase the heat to medium-high and bring to a boil. Cook for 1 minute to reduce the liquid slightly.

3. Add the mussels, cover, and cook until the mussels open, 5 to 8 minutes. Discard any unopened mussels.

4. Place the mussels in soup bowls and top with the chorizo mixture. Garnish with cilantro. Serve with crusty bread.

BLACK PEPPER SAKE MUSSELS
with Granny Smith Apples

THIS RECIPE IS A SPECIAL SHOWSTOPPER but can be prepared in minutes. Mussels are easy to find, inexpensive, and good for you, and this recipe is more interesting than the usual marinara or garlic-butter preparation.

---

2 TABLESPOONS GRAPESEED OIL

1 TABLESPOON MINCED GARLIC

3 LARGE SHALLOTS, THINLY SLICED

1 TABLESPOON COARSELY GROUND BLACK PEPPER

2 POUNDS MUSSELS, CLEANED AND DEBEARDED

KOSHER SALT AND FRESHLY GROUND BLACK PEPPER

1/2 CUP SAKE

2 GRANNY SMITH APPLES, UNPEELED, CORED, AND CUT INTO FINE STRIPS

4 TABLESPOONS CLARIFIED BUTTER

PINCH OF TOGARASHI OR OTHER HOT PEPPER, FOR GARNISH

1. Warm the pan over high heat, then add the oil. Add the garlic, shallots, and coarse black pepper, and stir-fry for 30 seconds. Add the mussels, and season with salt and pepper. Add the sake, deglaze the pan, and cover the pan. When the mussels have begun to open, about 3 minutes, add the apples and the butter. (Discard any mussels that haven't opened.)

2. Continue to cook until the flavors have combined, about 2 minutes. Sprinkle with the togarashi before serving.

PUMPKIN RISOTTO
with Sage and Cheese

PUMPKIN AND SAGE ARE PERFECT FLAVOR PARTNERS in this delicious side dish, or hearty vegetarian main course (if you use vegetable stock), that is made easy with your Simply Ming Stovetop Oven. The nonstick finish ensures that the rice won't stick, and cleanup is a breeze! Making risotto is a meditative process with a beautiful, impressive result, and this recipe is a great place to start if you're a beginner.

2 TABLESPOONS OLIVE OIL

7 OR 8 OUNCES SHALLOTS, MINCED

1 1/2 CUPS ARBORIO RICE

1/4 CUP DRY WHITE WINE, SUCH AS PINOT GRIGIO OR PINOT BIANCO

4 CUPS CUBED PUMPKIN, CUT INTO 1/2-INCH PIECES

3 1/2 CUPS REDUCED-SODIUM CHICKEN BROTH OR VEGETABLE STOCK

1/2 CUP (1 STICK) UNSALTED BUTTER

1 1/4 CUPS GRATED PARMESAN CHEESE

1/2 TEASPOON GROUND NUTMEG

6 TO 10 LARGE SAGE LEAVES, FINELY CHOPPED

KOSHER SALT AND FRESHLY GROUND BLACK PEPPER

1. Preheat the oven to 350°F. Warm the pan over medium heat, then add the oil. Add the shallots and cook, stirring, until they are translucent with a few brown edges, 6 to 7 minutes. Add the rice and stir until all the grains are coated with oil, 2 to 3 minutes. Reduce the heat to low. Add the wine and cook, stirring constantly, until it is absorbed.

2. Add the pumpkin and stock, and bring to a boil. Turn off the heat, put the lid (temperature gauge removed) on the pan, and place the pan in the oven. Bake for 25 to 35 minutes.

3. Remove from the oven, uncover, and gently stir in the butter, Parmesan, nutmeg, and sage.

4. Season with salt and pepper to taste.

Stovetop MACARONI AND CHEESE

THIS CLASSIC MACARONI AND CHEESE just happens to be made in one pot—the miraculously nonstick stovetop oven! You'll never go back to the box.

3½ TABLESPOONS CLARIFIED BUTTER

3 TABLESPOONS FLOUR

2 CUPS MILK

2½ CUPS WATER

1 TEASPOON GARLIC POWDER

½ TEASPOON ONION POWDER

½ TEASPOON MUSTARD POWDER

2½ CUPS ELBOW MACARONI, UNCOOKED

¾ CUP SHREDDED MOZZARELLA CHEESE

1½ CUPS SHREDDED CHEDDAR CHEESE

KOSHER SALT AND FRESHLY GROUND BLACK PEPPER

1. Warm the pan over medium heat, then add the butter. Add the flour and cook for 1 minute.

2. Slowly whisk the milk into the pan, a little at a time, until well combined. Mix in the water, garlic powder, onion powder, and mustard powder. Add the macaroni. When steam forms, reduce the heat to low. Cook for about 10 minutes, stirring occasionally, until the sauce thickens a bit and the macaroni is al dente. Remove from the heat.

3. Quickly stir in the mozzarella and Cheddar. Season with salt and pepper to taste.

Easy CHEDDAR-RICE FRITTATA

AS PERFECT FOR BREAKFAST AS IT IS FOR LUNCH or as a simple supper, this easy frittata can be thrown together with ingredients right from the fridge. If you don't have Cheddar, feel free to use Swiss or American or any other kind of cheese. You can spice it up with a jalapeño or cayenne pepper if you like a little heat.

---

4 EGGS

KOSHER SALT AND
FRESHLY GROUND BLACK
PEPPER

1 TABLESPOON
CLARIFIED BUTTER

1 SMALL ONION,
MINCED

1 CUP COOKED RICE

1 CUP GRATED
CHEDDAR CHEESE

1. Preheat the oven to 450°F.

2. In a medium bowl, whisk the eggs with a fork. Season with salt and pepper.

3. Warm the pan over medium-high heat, then add the butter. Add the onion and sauté until soft, about 5 minutes.

4. Add the rice and season with salt and pepper, then add the eggs. Mix quickly, add the Cheddar, mix quickly again, and place in the oven.

5. Cook until the eggs start to puff and brown, about 2 minutes.

Shiitake BROWN RICE PILAF

A PERFECT MEATLESS MAIN DISH or a fantastic side dish with any kind of roasted or grilled meat, this rice pilaf also makes a great lunch the next day. Feel free to use any kind of mushrooms you like—we use shiitake here, but regular button mushrooms work just fine.

2 TABLESPOONS OLIVE OIL

1 TABLESPOON MINCED GARLIC

1 CUP MINCED SHALLOT

2 CUPS BROWN RICE

KOSHER SALT AND FRESHLY GROUND BLACK PEPPER

4 CUPS REDUCED-SODIUM CHICKEN STOCK

1 CINNAMON STICK

2 CUPS SHIITAKE MUSHROOMS, STEMMED AND SLICED

1 BAY LEAF

1. Rinse the rice and soak in cold water for 1 hour. Drain in a colander until dry.

2. Preheat the oven to 350°F.

3. Warm the pan over medium heat, then add the oil. Add the garlic and shallots and cook for about 30 seconds, until the aroma and oils are released. Add the rice and season with salt and pepper. Cook for 1 to 2 minutes, until the rice is golden brown. Add the stock, cinnamon stick, mushrooms, and bay leaf, and bring to a simmer. Scrape the grains of rice from the side of the pot to prevent burning. Remove from the heat.

4. Cover the pan with the lid (temperature gauge removed), place in the oven, and cook until all the liquid is absorbed, 20 to 25 minutes. Discard the cinnamon stick and bay leaf.

50/50
WHITE AND BROWN RICE

CAN'T DECIDE WHETHER YOU WANT white or brown rice? Make both! This 50/50 rice is a Ming Tsai classic, and for good reason. Keep a batch on hand to use in simple fried rice dishes or even as stuffing.

1½ CUPS BROWN RICE   1½ CUPS WHITE RICE

1. Rinse the brown rice and let it soak in cold water to cover for about 1 hour.

2. In a medium bowl, rinse the white rice by filling the bowl with water and stirring by hand. Drain and repeat until the water in the bowl is clear.

3. Add both the brown and the white rice to the pan. Flatten the rice with your palm and without removing your hand, add water until it touches the highest knuckle of your middle finger.

4. Cover and boil over high heat for 10 minutes.

5. Reduce the heat to medium and simmer for 30 minutes. Turn off the heat, cover, and let the rice stand to plump, 20 minutes. Stir gently before serving.

DELICIOUS DESSERTS

RICH CHOCOLATE PUDDING *Topped with Hazelnuts*

IF YOU GO CRAZY FOR CHOCOLATE-hazelnut spread, try this decadent pudding with a similar flavor profile. Although the pudding is not hard to make, you can prepare it ahead for a special event—the pudding will last, covered in the fridge, for up to 4 days.

3 CUPS COCONUT MILK

2 LARGE EGG YOLKS

1 CUP SUGAR

¼ CUP CORNSTARCH

2 TABLESPOONS UNSWEETENED COCOA POWDER

PINCH OF KOSHER SALT

8 OUNCES DARK CHOCOLATE, COARSELY CHOPPED

2 TABLESPOONS UNSALTED BUTTER

2 TEASPOONS VANILLA EXTRACT

1 CUP CHOPPED ROASTED HAZELNUTS

EDIBLE GERANIUM LEAF, FOR GARNISH (OPTIONAL)

1. In a small bowl, whisk together the coconut milk and egg yolks.

2. Warm the pan over medium heat. Combine the sugar, cornstarch, cocoa powder, salt, and chocolate in a bowl, then add to the pan. Follow by streaming in the milk-egg mixture, whisking constantly until the mixture is smooth. Bring to a low boil for 1 minute until thickened. Remove from the heat and whisk in the butter and vanilla.

3. Divide the pudding among 4 cups, cover each with plastic wrap, and refrigerate to cool. Top with the chopped hazelnuts. Garnish with a geranium leaf (if using).

Simple From-Scratch
BUTTERSCOTCH PUDDING

BUTTERSCOTCH PUDDING IS A CLASSIC, and it's super simple to make your own in minutes. Forget the box, and grab these basic ingredients that transform into creamy magic when they meet your stovetop oven!

1 CUP PACKED DARK BROWN SUGAR

1/4 CUP CORNSTARCH

1/2 TEASPOON KOSHER SALT

2 TABLESPOONS UNSALTED BUTTER

2 1/2 CUPS MILK

1/2 CUP HEAVY CREAM

3 EGG YOLKS, BEATEN

1 TEASPOON VANILLA EXTRACT

1. In a small bowl, mix together the brown sugar, cornstarch, and salt. Set aside.

2. Warm the pan over medium heat, then melt the butter. Reduce the heat to low, add the brown sugar mixture, and cook, stirring frequently, for 1 to 2 minutes. Slowly whisk in the milk and heavy cream. Bring to a gentle simmer for 1 minute.

3. Place the egg yolks in a small bowl. Temper the yolks by quickly stirring in about 1/4 cup of the hot milk mixture. Pour the yolk mixture into the pan. Cook, stirring constantly, for 1 minute. Remove from the heat, and stir in the vanilla. Pour into bowls, and let cool slightly.

Creamy
COCONUT PUDDING

COCONUT IS A TRENDY FLAVOR right now—for good reason. Who doesn't love a little tropical vibe? You can enjoy it in a simple, luscious pudding that only takes minutes of hands-on time in the kitchen.

1 1/2 CUPS SUGAR

1 CUP UNSWEETENED SHREDDED COCONUT

1 CUP HEAVY CREAM, DIVIDED

2 EGGS

1 CUP COCONUT MILK

8 OUNCES CREAM CHEESE, CUT INTO PIECES

2 TEASPOONS COCONUT EXTRACT

1/2 TEASPOON VANILLA EXTRACT

1. In a large microwavable bowl, combine the sugar, coconut, and 1/2 cup of the heavy cream. Microwave on HIGH for 1 minute. Set aside.

2. In another bowl, combine the remaining 1/2 cup heavy cream and the eggs. Beat until thoroughly combined. Set aside.

3. Warm the pan over medium heat. Add the coconut milk and cream cheese and whisk slowly, about 5 minutes, until the cream cheese has melted. Add the coconut mixture and the egg mixture, and continue whisking as the pudding cooks, about 5 minutes, until bubbles form at the edge of the pan and the pudding begins to thicken. Remove from the heat, and stir in the coconut extract and vanilla. Transfer the mixture to a large bowl. Let cool a bit, then cover and refrigerate for at least 4 hours or preferably overnight.

BLACKBERRY CRUMBLE
with Vanilla Ice Cream

CRUMBLES GIVE YOU ALL THE FLAVOR of a pie without all the prep work and time in the kitchen. If you like your topping a bit more brown, finish your dish with just a few quick minutes under the broiler.

4 TO 5 CUPS FRESH OR FROZEN BLACKBERRIES

1/4 CUP GRANULATED SUGAR

CRUMBLE
2 CUPS FLOUR

2 CUPS ROLLED OATS

1 1/2 CUPS PACKED LIGHT BROWN SUGAR

1 TEASPOON GROUND CINNAMON

1 CUP UNSALTED BUTTER, CUT INTO PIECES

VANILLA ICE CREAM, FOR TOPPING

MINT, FOR GARNISH

1. Preheat the oven to 350°F.

2. In a small bowl, toss the berries with the granulated sugar. Set aside.

3. To make the crumble: In a medium bowl, combine the flour, oats, brown sugar, and cinnamon. Cut the butter into the mixture until crumbly.

4. In the slightly oiled or buttered pan, sprinkle enough crumble to cover the bottom. Add the berries. Top with the remaining crumble.

5. Bake for 40 minutes or until the crumble is golden brown. Scoop into bowls and top with the ice cream. Garnish with mint leaves.

Toasty S'MORES DIP

ENJOY THE GOOEY GOODNESS of s'mores even when you can't have a campfire. Chocolate and marshmallow meld together and toast up beautifully right in your stovetop oven. Don't forget the graham crackers for dipping!

½ TABLESPOON UNSALTED BUTTER

1½ CUPS CHOCOLATE CHIPS (SEMISWEET, MILK CHOCOLATE, OR A COMBO)

15 JUMBO MARSHMALLOWS, HALVED

GRAHAM CRACKER SQUARES OR STICKS

1. Preheat the oven to 450°F with the pan inside.

2. Remove the pan from the oven, then add the butter and swirl to coat the bottom and sides. Add the chocolate chips in an even layer, then arrange marshmallow halves on top, cut-side down, covering the chocolate completely.

3. Bake for 5 to 7 minutes or until the marshmallows are toasted. Remove from the oven and allow to rest for 5 minutes. Serve with graham cracker squares or sticks.

Dark Chocolate
MOCHA BROWNIES

THE AROMA OF BROWNIES IN THE OVEN: It's a favorite memory. Make memories tonight with these rich treats that glide out of the stovetop oven.

1¹/₃ CUPS FLOUR

2 TEASPOONS
BAKING POWDER

2 TEASPOONS INSTANT
COFFEE GRANULES

1 TEASPOON
KOSHER SALT

1 CUP BUTTER,
AT ROOM TEMPERATURE

2 CUPS GRANULATED
SUGAR

4 EGGS

1 TEASPOON
VANILLA EXTRACT

7 TO 8 OUNCES DARK
CHOCOLATE, MELTED AND
SLIGHTLY COOLED

POWDERED SUGAR,
FOR TOPPING

MINT, FOR GARNISH

1. Preheat the oven to 350°F.

2. In a medium bowl, combine the flour, baking powder, instant coffee, and salt. Set aside.

3. In a large bowl with a handheld mixer, beat the butter and granulated sugar until light and fluffy. Beat in the eggs, then add the vanilla.

4. Gradually add the flour mixture to the butter mixture. Add the chocolate, and stir until just combined.

5. Spread the batter into a buttered or oiled pan. Bake for 30 to 35 minutes. Dust with powdered sugar. Garnish with mint leaves.

Perfect Pan
PEACH COBBLER

PEACHES ARE A COBBLER CLASSIC—their juicy sweetness really sings when baked. But feel free to experiment with other fruits in this indispensable cobbler recipe—your Simply Ming Stovetop Oven can handle anything! Just adjust the cooking time as needed.

FILLING

8 FRESH PEACHES, PEELED, PITTED, AND SLICED

1/4 CUP GRANULATED SUGAR

1/4 CUP LIGHT BROWN SUGAR

1/2 TEASPOON GROUND CINNAMON

1/8 TEASPOON GROUND NUTMEG

1 TABLESPOON FRESH LEMON JUICE

1/2 TEASPOON VANILLA EXTRACT

2 TEASPOONS CORNSTARCH

TOPPING

1 CUP FLOUR

1/4 CUP PLUS 3 TABLESPOONS GRANULATED SUGAR, DIVIDED

1/4 CUP LIGHT BROWN SUGAR

1 TEASPOON BAKING POWDER

1/2 TEASPOON SALT

6 TABLESPOONS UNSALTED BUTTER, CHILLED AND CUT INTO SMALL PIECES

1/4 CUP BOILING WATER

1 TEASPOON GROUND CINNAMON

1/3 CUP SLICED ALMONDS (OPTIONAL)

VANILLA ICE CREAM, FOR SERVING

1. Preheat the oven to 425°F.

2. To make the filling: In a large bowl, combine the peaches, granulated sugar, brown sugar, cinnamon, nutmeg, lemon juice, vanilla, and cornstarch. Toss to coat the peaches. Transfer to the pan, and bake for 10 minutes.

3. To make the topping: In a medium bowl, combine the flour, 1/4 cup of the granulated sugar, brown sugar, baking powder, and salt. Cut in the butter until the mixture is crumbly. Stir in the boiling water until just combined.

4. In a small bowl, combine the remaining 3 tablespoons granulated sugar with the cinnamon.

5. Remove the peaches from the oven. Spoon the topping over the peaches, then sprinkle on the cinnamon-sugar mixture and sliced almonds (if using). Return the pan to the oven to bake for 25 to 35 minutes or until the topping is golden brown. Serve warm with vanilla ice cream.

APPLE CAKE
with Walnut Streusel Topping

SO MANY WAYS TO ENJOY! Savor this delicious, moist apple cake just as it bakes up, warm from the oven. Or take the taste to a new level by topping with Creamy Salted Caramel Sauce (page 150) and whipped cream.

STREUSEL TOPPING

3/4 CUP UNSALTED BUTTER

2/3 CUP SUGAR

3 1/2 LARGE GOLDEN DELICIOUS APPLES, PEELED, CORED, AND QUARTERED

1/2 CUP COARSELY CHOPPED WALNUTS

APPLE CAKE

1 1/2 CUPS FLOUR

1 1/2 TEASPOONS BAKING POWDER

3/4 TEASPOON KOSHER SALT

1/2 TEASPOON GROUND CINNAMON

1/2 CUP UNSALTED BUTTER, SOFTENED

2/3 CUP SUGAR

1 TEASPOON VANILLA EXTRACT

2 TABLESPOONS MINCED FRESH GINGER

2 LARGE EGGS

1/2 CUP SOUR CREAM

1/2 GOLDEN DELICIOUS APPLE, PEELED, CORED, AND FINELY CHOPPED

1. To make the streusel topping: Warm the pan over low heat, then melt the butter (butter should not separate). Stir in the sugar until well combined. Arrange the apple quarters, cut-sides up, in the pan and sprinkle the walnuts evenly in between the apples. Cook the mixture, undisturbed, for 25 to 35 minutes, or until the apples are tender in the center and the sugar is a golden caramel.

2. Preheat the oven to 375°F.

3. To make the cake: In a bowl, whisk together the flour, baking powder, salt, and cinnamon. Set aside. In another bowl, with an electric mixer, beat the butter and sugar until light and fluffy. Beat in the vanilla and ginger. Add the eggs, one at a time, beating well after each addition. Beat in the sour cream. With the mixer on low speed, beat in the flour mixture gradually until just combined. Fold the chopped apple into the batter.

4. Remove the pan from the heat and spoon the cake batter evenly over the topping. With a metal spatula, spread the batter (being careful not to disturb the topping), leaving a ¼-inch border of cooked apples uncovered. Put the pan in a shallow baking dish and bake in the middle of the oven for 25 to 35 minutes or until the cake is golden brown. Cool the cake in the pan on a rack for 10 minutes. Carefully loosen around the edges and invert the cake onto a plate.

Creamy Salted
CARAMEL SAUCE

IT'S ALSO KNOWN AS LIQUID GOLD, and you can make it right in your kitchen to top everything from cakes and cupcakes to ice cream and coffee drinks. The Simply Ming pan makes it easy to enjoy any time! Whip up a batch and refrigerate the sauce for up to 2 weeks; just warm it in 5-second intervals in the microwave before using.

2 CUPS SUGAR

3/4 CUP UNSALTED
BUTTER, AT ROOM
TEMPERATURE AND
CUT INTO PIECES

1 CUP HEAVY CREAM,
AT ROOM TEMPERATURE

1 TABLESPOON
SEA SALT

1. Warm the pan over medium-high heat, then melt the sugar, swirling the pan frequently. As soon as the sugar turns amber, whisk in the butter until melted.

2. Remove the pan from the heat and slowly pour in the cream while whisking vigorously until all the cream is incorporated. Whisk in the sea salt.

3. Serve immediately or pour into a heat-safe container to cool completely and store.

Homemade HOT FUDGE SAUCE

WHY SETTLE FOR STOREBOUGHT when homemade fudgy goodness is as simple as this? A good hot fudge recipe works as the finishing touch for so many favorite desserts. So, go ahead and indulge with a little help from the Simply Ming Stovetop Oven.

½ CUP SALTED BUTTER, CUT INTO PIECES

⅓ CUP UNSWEETENED COCOA POWDER

⅔ CUP MILK CHOCOLATE CHIPS

2 CUPS SUGAR

1 CAN (12 OUNCES) EVAPORATED MILK

1 TEASPOON VANILLA EXTRACT

1. Warm the pan over medium-low heat. Add the butter, cocoa powder, chocolate chips, sugar, and evaporated milk. Stir to combine. Increase the heat to medium-high and bring to a boil. Immediately reduce the heat to low and continue simmering for 7 minutes, stirring constantly.

2. Remove from the heat and add the vanilla.

3. Serve immediately or pour into a heat-safe container to cool completely and store.

12-Inch CHOCOLATE CHIP COOKIE

SAVE TIME AND BAKING SHEETS with this sweet take on a favorite cookie. So much simpler than shaping all those little cookies—and perfect for topping with ice cream, like an amazing chocolate chip cookie pie!

2 CUPS FLOUR

1 TEASPOON BAKING SODA

3/4 TEASPOON KOSHER SALT

3/4 CUP UNSALTED BUTTER, SOFTENED

1/2 CUP GRANULATED SUGAR

3/4 CUP PACKED LIGHT BROWN SUGAR

1 LARGE EGG, AT ROOM TEMPERATURE

2 TEASPOONS VANILLA EXTRACT

1 1/2 CUPS CHOCOLATE CHIPS

1 1/2 CUPS CHOPPED PECANS

ICE CREAM, FOR TOPPING (OPTIONAL)

1. Preheat the oven to 350°F.

2. In a medium bowl, combine the flour, baking soda, and salt. Set aside.

3. In a large bowl or the work bowl of an electric mixer, beat the butter, granulated sugar, and brown sugar until light and fluffy. Add the egg and vanilla and beat until fully incorporated. Add the flour mixture and beat just until the flour is incorporated. Stir in the chocolate chips and pecans.

4. Oil or butter the pan, then add the cookie dough in an even layer. Bake for 30 to 40 minutes, until puffed and golden with browned edges. Allow to cool on a wire rack for about 20 minutes. Cut into wedges to serve. Top with ice cream, if desired.

Nutty
CHOCOLATE FUDGE

MAKE ANY DAY A SPECIAL OCCASION by whipping up a batch of chocolate fudge. Your Simply Ming Stovetop Oven works hard for you to give you amazing results—and amazingly little cleanup. So, surprise your loved ones today!

2½ CUPS SUGAR

¼ CUP UNSALTED BUTTER

1 CAN (6 OUNCES) EVAPORATED MILK

6 OUNCES SEMISWEET CHOCOLATE CHIPS

½ CUP CHOPPED PECANS OR WALNUTS

1 TEASPOON VANILLA EXTRACT

1. Warm the pan over medium heat. Add the sugar, butter, and milk. Stir and bring to a boil. Reduce the heat to low and simmer for 6 minutes, stirring occasionally.

2. Remove from the heat. Add the chocolate chips and chopped nuts. Stir until the fudge begins to form. Then quickly stir in the vanilla.

3. Let cool, then cut into pieces.

GIANT CINNAMON ROLL
with Cream Cheese Icing

YOU MAY NEVER BAKE SINGLE CINNAMON ROLLS AGAIN once you've made this soft and flaky pastry filled with cinnamon-sugar goodness and topped with cream cheese icing! It's easy and just plain fun to make and serve. And the giant roll makes quite an impression when entertaining.

DOUGH

1 CUP MILK

1/2 CUP PLUS 1 TEASPOON GRANULATED SUGAR, DIVIDED

1 TEASPOON KOSHER SALT

1 CUP WARM WATER

4 1/2 TEASPOONS (2 PACKETS) ACTIVE DRY YEAST

2 EGGS, AT ROOM TEMPERATURE

6 CUPS FLOUR

1/4 CUP UNSALTED BUTTER, MELTED

FILLING

1/2 CUP GRANULATED SUGAR

1/2 CUP LIGHT BROWN SUGAR

1 TABLESPOON GROUND CINNAMON

1/2 CUP UNSALTED BUTTER, AT ROOM TEMPERATURE

ICING

8 OUNCES CREAM CHEESE, SOFTENED

1/2 CUP UNSALTED BUTTER, SOFTENED

1/2 CUP SOUR CREAM

1 TEASPOON VANILLA EXTRACT

8 CUPS POWDERED SUGAR

1. To make the dough: In a small saucepan, warm the milk, 1/2 cup of the granulated sugar, and salt over medium-high heat. Stir until the sugar melts and a few small bubbles appear at the edges. Remove from the heat and let cool.

2. In a large bowl, add the warm water to the yeast and the remaining 1 teaspoon granulated sugar. Let stand for 10 minutes.

3. Beat the eggs into the yeast mixture. Stir in the (now lukewarm) milk mixture. Beat in the flour a little at a time until the dough is elastic. Add the melted butter and mix, then add in more flour. (The dough should be elastic but a bit sticky.) Turn the dough out onto a lightly floured surface and knead for 10 minutes. Place in a buttered or oiled bowl, cover, and let rise in a warm spot for about 1 hour or until doubled.

4. To make the filling: In a small bowl, combine the granulated sugar, brown sugar, and cinnamon. Set aside.

5. On a lightly floured surface, roll the dough into a large rectangle about ¼ inch thick. Spread on the butter, then sprinkle with the cinnamon-sugar mixture. Cut the dough into 2-inch strips.

6. Oil the pan, then start by rolling one strip to form the middle; place in the pan. Take each strip of dough and wrap around the center piece in the pan. When all the dough has been used, cover and let it rise, for about 45 minutes or until doubled.

7. Preheat the oven to 400°F.

8. Put the pan into the oven. Bake for 25 to 35 minutes or until golden brown.

9. To make the icing: In the work bowl of an electric mixer, beat the cream cheese and butter until fluffy. Beat in the sour cream and vanilla. With the mixer on low, slowly add the powdered sugar.

10. Spread the cinnamon roll with the icing. Slice like a cake to serve.

RICOTTA-FILLED CREPES *with Blueberries*

BREAKFAST OR DESSERT? You decide—crepes can step into either role. Luscious ricotta and cream cheese make this a richer crepe recipe, while blueberries satisfy your sweet tooth. But if you enjoy it for breakfast, we won't tell!

---

1 CUP RICOTTA CHEESE

1 TABLESPOON LEMON ZEST (OPTIONAL)

4 OUNCES CREAM CHEESE

4 EGGS

1/4 CUP SUGAR

PINCH OF SALT

DASH OF GROUND CINNAMON

3 TABLESPOONS UNSALTED BUTTER, DIVIDED

1 PINT BLUEBERRIES

1. In the work bowl of a food processor, whirl the ricotta and lemon zest (if using) until smooth and fluffy. Transfer the ricotta to a bowl and scrape out the work bowl. Add the cream cheese, eggs, sugar, salt, and cinnamon to the work bowl and process until smooth.

2. Warm the pan over medium-high heat, then melt 1 teaspoon of the butter. Pour about 2 tablespoons of the cream cheese/egg mixture into the pan and tilt it so that the batter evenly coats the bottom. Cook for 1 to 2 minutes until the top is set.

Flip the crepe and cook for another 30 seconds until it begins to brown. Transfer the crepe to a plate. Repeat with the butter and remaining cream cheese/egg mixture.

3. Spread about 2 tablespoons of the ricotta in the center of a crepe and roll it up, placing it seam-side down on a serving plate. Repeat with the remaining ricotta mixture and crepes. Scatter the berries on top of the crepes and serve.

Old-Fashioned
CARAMEL APPLES

NOW YOU CAN ENJOY THE CARNIVAL TREAT anytime. Don't let fear of mess scare you—everything comes together easily and cleans up just as easily with the Simply Ming pan. Make it a fun evening with a fair-style indulgence!

1/2 CUP WATER

1 1/3 CUPS PACKED LIGHT BROWN SUGAR

1 TEASPOON KOSHER SALT

1 CUP PLUS 2 TABLESPOONS HEAVY CREAM

8 TO 12 SMALL APPLES

ASSORTED TOPPINGS, SUCH AS CHOPPED NUTS, SPRINKLES, OR MELTED CHOCOLATE

1. Warm the pan over medium heat. Add the water, brown sugar, and salt. Stir until the brown sugar is fully dissolved and forms a syrup. Bring to a rolling boil, about 4 minutes. Simmer, without stirring, until the syrup is golden, about 9 minutes. Immediately add the heavy cream and reduce the heat to medium-low, stirring constantly, until a caramel forms and registers 248°F on a candy thermometer, about 7 minutes. Transfer to a small heat-resistant bowl and cool to about 212°F.

2. Skewer the apples with Popsicle sticks.

3. Dip the apples into the caramel, letting excess drip off before transferring to a parchment-lined platter. Top with nuts or sprinkles, or drizzle with melted chocolate. Let stand at room temperature until fully set, about 10 minutes.

ALPHABETICAL LIST OF RECIPES

Almond Butter Stuffed French Toast, 36

Andouille Sausage and Shrimp
   Jambalaya, 108

Apple Cake with Walnut
   Streusel Topping, 148

Apple-Cinnamon Breakfast Bowl, 44

Asian Shrimp Lettuce Wraps, 27

Bacon and Tomato Avocado Toast, 45

Bacon-Wrapped Avocado Bites, 20

Beer-Steamed Mussels with Chorizo, 128

Bell Peppers Stuffed with
   Spicy Pork Fried Rice, 96

Black Bean Breakfast Skillet, 52

Black Pepper Sake Mussels
   with Granny Smith Apples, 129

Blackberry Crumble with
   Vanilla Ice Cream, 143

Breakfast Stuffed Peppers, 33

Brined Roast Chicken, 66

Cheesy Spinach-Artichoke Dip, 8

Chili-Lime Shrimp Skewers, 14

Chunky Beef Ragu, 100

Classic Beef Stew with Red Wine, 102

Classic Bolognese Sauce, 89

Coconut Chicken Curry, 60

Creamy Coconut Pudding, 141

Creamy Garlic Shrimp Risotto, 112

Creamy Sage Sausage Gravy, 57

Creamy Salted Caramel Sauce, 150

Dark Chocolate–Maple Quinoa, 35

Dark Chocolate Mocha Brownies, 145

Easy Cheddar-Rice Frittata, 133

Easy Chicken Tortilla Soup, 76

Egg and Chorizo Breakfast Burrito, 40

50/50 White and Brown Rice, 135

Foolproof Spaghetti Carbonara, 86

French Toast Sticks with Apple Dip, 39

Fried Egg Sandwich with Spinach, 54

Game-Day Beef and Beer Chili, 101

Garden Vegetable Frittata, 48

Giant Cinnamon Roll
   with Cream Cheese Icing, 154

Ginger Braised Whole Chicken, 64

Ginger Chicken Thighs with Parsnips, 65

Ginger-Orange Duck "Cassoulet," 81

Greek Egg and Lemon Soup with Orzo, 78

Grown-Up Sloppy Joes, 106

Ham and Mushroom Pizza Omelet, 30

Homemade Hot Fudge Sauce, 151

Homemade Sage Sausage, 56

Honey-Glazed Grilled Pineapple, 22

Just-Like-Mom's Ricotta Meatballs, 99

Moroccan Lamb Stew, 83

Mozzarella Eggplant Stacks, 26

New England Clam Chowder, 126

New Orleans Style Chicken
   and Sausage Gumbo, 70

Nutty Chocolate Fudge, 153

Old-Fashioned Caramel Apples, 157

Olive Oil–Poached Salmon
    with Tomato Tapenade, 122

One-Pan Chicken Alfredo Pasta, 73

One-Pan Chicken Cacciatore, 63

One-Pan Teriyaki Salmon, 120

Orange-Ginger Lamb Shanks
    with Garlic Barley Risotto, 84

Parmesan Zucchini Crisps, 24

Peppered Pork Tenderloin with Sweet
    and Sour Cranberry-Coconut Sauce, 92

Perfect Pan Peach Cobbler, 146

Pork Tenderloin with Maple Glaze, 93

Pumpkin Crepes with Berry Jam, 51

Pumpkin Risotto with Sage
    and Cheese, 130

Red Pepper and Asparagus Quesadillas, 23

Red Roast Duck Legs with
    Sweet Potatoes and Daikon, 80

Rich Chocolate Pudding Topped
    with Hazelnuts, 138

Ricotta-Filled Crepes with Blueberries, 156

Roast Turkey Breast Porchetta Style, 74

Roasted Chicken Provençal, 72

Roasted Red Pepper Dip, 25

Salmon Pasta with Cherry
    Tomato Sauce, 123

Savory Shrimp Lobster Boil, 118

Scallop Caprese Stacks, 11

Shiitake Brown Rice Pilaf, 134

Short Ribs with Root Vegetables, 98

Shrimp Scampi Over Spaghetti, 111

Simple Chicken Yakitori, 13

Simple From-Scratch
    Butterscotch Pudding, 140

Simple Pulled Pork, 90

Simple Shakshouka, 43

Skillet Smoky Salsa, 18

Smoked Jerk Chicken, 68

Spaghetti alle Vongole, 125

Spice-Rubbed BBQ Ribs, 94

Stovetop Macaroni and Cheese, 132

Stovetop Ropa Vieja, 105

Sweet Potato and Sausage Frittata, 32

Sweet Potato Hash with
    Egg and Spinach, 49

Tea-Smoked Salmon, 119

Teriyaki Shrimp Stir-Fry, 114

Thai Salmon Sliders, 21

Thai Scrambled Eggs, 53

Thai Shrimp Soup, 117

Toasty S'mores Dip, 144

12-Inch Chocolate Chip Cookie, 152

Veal Stew with Sweet Peppers, 82

Vegetable Stuffed Mushrooms, 17

Very Berry Puff Pancake, 34

Warm French Onion Dip, 10

Zesty Breakfast Potatoes, 46

METRIC CONVERSIONS

VOLUME

US	METRIC
1/8 TEASPOON	0.5 MILLILITERS
1/4 TEASPOON	1 MILLILITERS
1/2 TEASPOON	2 MILLILITERS
3/4 TEASPOON	4 MILLILITERS
1 TEASPOON	5 MILLILITERS
1 TABLESPOON	15 MILLILITERS
1/4 CUP	60 MILLILITERS
1/3 CUP	80 MILLILITERS
1/2 CUP	120 MILLILITERS
2/3 CUP	160 MILLILITERS
3/4 CUP	180 MILLILITERS
1 CUP	225 MILLILITERS (DRY), 250 MILLILITERS (LIQUID)
2 CUPS (1 PINT)	450 MILLILITERS (DRY), 500 MILLILITERS (LIQUID)
4 CUPS (1 QUART)	1 LITER
1/2 GALLON	2 LITERS
1 GALLON	4 LITERS

WEIGHT

US	METRIC
1 OUNCE	28 GRAMS
4 OUNCES (1/4 POUND)	113 GRAMS
8 OUNCES (1/2 POUND)	230 GRAMS
12 OUNCES (3/4 POUND)	340 GRAMS
16 OUNCES (1 POUND)	450 GRAMS
23 OUNCES (2 POUNDS)	900 GRAMS

LENGTH

US	METRIC
1/4 INCH	6 MILLIMETERS
1/2 INCH	13 MILLIMETERS
3/4 INCH	19 MILLIMETERS
1 INCH	2 1/2 CENTIMETERS
1 1/2 INCHES	3 3/4 CENTIMETERS
2 INCHES	5 CENTIMETERS
2 1/2 INCHES	6 1/2 CENTIMETERS

TEMPERATURES

FAHRENHEIT	CELSIUS
250°F	120°C
275°F	140°C
300°F	150°C
325°F	170°C
350°F	180°C
375°F	190°C
400°F	200°C
425°F	220°C
450°F	230°C
475°F	240°C
500°F	260°C